General
Fire Hazards
and
Fire Prevention

General
Fire Hazards
and
Fire Prevention

J. J. WILLIAMSON
F.C.I.I., F.I.A.S.

SIXTH EDITION

PITMAN PUBLISHING

First edition 1943
Second edition 1944
Reprinted 1946
Third edition 1951
Revised and reprinted 1954
Fourth edition 1958
Reprinted 1961
Fifth edition 1965
Reprinted 1966
Sixth edition 1971
First paperback edition 1971
Reprinted 1972

SIR ISAAC PITMAN AND SONS LTD
Pitman House, Parker Street, Kingsway, London, WC2B 5PB
P.O. Box 46038, Portal Street, Nairobi, Kenya

SIR ISAAC PITMAN (AUST.) PTY. LTD
Pitman House, 158 Bouverie Street, Carlton, Victoria 3053, Australia

PITMAN PUBLISHING COMPANY S.A. LTD
P.O. Box 11231, Johannesburg, South Africa

PITMAN PUBLISHING CORPORATION
6 East 43rd Street, New York, N.Y. 10017, U.S.A.

SIR ISAAC PITMAN (CANADA) LTD
495 Wellington Street West, Toronto 135, Canada

THE COPP CLARK PUBLISHING COMPANY
517 Wellington Street West, Toronto 135, Canada

©
J. J. Williamson
1965, 1971

Cased edition ISBN 0 273 31539 0
Paperback edition ISBN 0 273 36056 6

Text set in 10 pt. Monotype Old Style, printed by letterpress,
and bound in Great Britain at The Pitman Press, Bath
G2–(B853/B1042:43)

THE
CHARTERED INSURANCE
INSTITUTE

INSURANCE HANDBOOK No. 8

This Handbook is issued under the authority of
THE CHARTERED INSURANCE INSTITUTE and is
designed specially for the use of students.

PREFACE TO SIXTH EDITION

THE chapters on building construction have been entirely re-written and the other parts revised in the light of recent developments, particularly the Building Regulations 1965. The opportunity has been taken to bring the text into accord with modern usage, for example by stating temperatures on the Centigrade scale. Linear measurements have not been changed to Metric because most of the authorities have not yet decided whether to use exact equivalents, which would be unwieldly, or to adopt approximations such as 300 mm for 1 foot and 25 mm for 1 inch.

LONDON   J. J. W.

PREFACE TO THE FIRST EDITION

THE subject of Fire Hazards and Fire Prevention has always been a prominent one in the curriculum of the student of fire insurance, and now that it is more generally understood that all loss by fire is a national loss the subject has an appeal to a very much wider circle.

Whilst the primary purpose of this book is to cover the Chartered Insurance Institute's Syllabus for "General Fire Hazards," it is hoped that it will also be useful to students and members of the Institution of Fire Engineers and to many others who are interested in Fire Prevention. With this objective the various hazards and their means of prevention are presented as simply and concisely as is consistent with enabling them to be thoroughly understood. Information, however interesting, which did not seem essential to this purpose has been omitted. Those who desire a deeper knowledge of various aspects will find on page 158 a list of books and published papers, to the authors of which I express acknowledgment of my obligation for information obtained from their work.

I am indebted to the Fire Offices Committee for permission to publish their rules for Standards II and V Construction.

My grateful thanks are due to Mr. D. Walker, A.C.I.I., who has been good enough to read through the proofs, and to my wife, who has given me considerable assistance.

J. J. W.

LONDON

CONTENTS

CHAPTER I

FIRES: THEIR CAUSES, DETECTION, AND EXTINGUISHMENT

THE loss of property directly caused by fire in this country is currently more than £100,000,000 annually and increases from year to year; but this is not the total of the loss. To the loss by fire, smoke, and water must be added the consequential loss—the interruption of business and production, and the loss occasioned by injury and illness. Although the amounts of these losses are difficult to compute, it is clear that the total is an impressive one.

It is not always appreciated that all loss by fire is a loss to the nation. When an individual loser is indemnified by insurance the effect is merely to spread the loss over a number of persons; the labour expended in replacing the property is a national loss, as it could otherwise have been employed in adding to the national wealth instead of merely replacing fire wastage. The minimization of loss by fire can, therefore, be regarded as a national duty, and it is surprising that until recently so little effort has been made to reduce this waste.

The problems of avoiding the outbreak of fires and of preventing their spread are studied in insurance circles under the heading of "Fire Hazards," but the subject is known to the Fire Service as "Fire Prevention" or "Fire Protection." The two designations are easily reconciled, for without an accurate and comprehensive knowledge of the hazards involved it is not possible to prevent fires; on the other hand a full knowledge of them usually suggests the remedy.

FIRE HAZARDS

"Fire Hazards" is a term which includes not only the causes of fires but embraces those circumstances which increase the probability of a fire occurring, or which enable or permit fires, once started, to spread and increase the loss. The cause of a fire is often given as "light thrown down," but it is obvious that the light would not have caused a fire had it not fallen where there was combustible material. Had it fallen in and ignited a heap of waste matter the loss would still have been negligible had there been no combustible materials near to extend the fire. Suppose, however, that a lighted match fell upon and ignited a heap of waste rags and shavings which in turn ignited a timber partition against which the waste was stacked; that the fire spread by way of flammable materials over the whole of the floor and, via open wood stairs, to other floors, until the whole of the building was involved. In such a case the loss directly attributable to the "cause of fire" would be negligible, but the features which spread the fire, i.e. the timber partition, the flammable stocks, and the open stairs would have increased the negligible loss to a very substantial one.

Fire hazards are generally regarded in two categories: firstly common hazards, which are those likely to be found in almost any premises—ordinary everyday hazards—and secondly, special hazards, which are those peculiar to or directly associated with particular occupancies. There can be no clear line of demarcation between the two, as processes limited to one trade may in time spread to others, e.g. the use of cellulose solutions was at one time practically confined to makers of "leather-cloth," but cellulose paints are now used in a large variety of trades. The term "General Fire Hazards" embraces the hazards of many such processes in addition to common hazards. Consideration of danger to life is excluded, yet it is clear that in preventing fires the possibilities of loss of life by fire are reduced.

DEFINITION OF FIRE

Fire or combustion is a chemical reaction, the combination of a substance with oxygen, by which heat is evolved. The reaction will not commence until the substance has been heated, but when it has started it will itself provide the heat to enable the fire to continue. Thus, there are three essentials for fire—fuel, oxygen and heat. A fire will not start unless heat, usually termed the "cause of fire", is supplied and it will go out if any of the three essentials is removed.

CAUSES OF FIRES

Many outbreaks of fire are not observed until so late that the cause is uncertain but, as the supposed source of ignition of every fire attended by a fire brigade in this country is reported, it is possible to obtain a reasonable knowledge of the frequency of the various sources.

The reports of the Joint Fire Research Organization indicate that the most common sources of ignition of fires in buildings are electrical installations and appliances, smoking materials and children playing with matches. Other sources include gas, oil, solid fuel, liquefied petroleum gas and acetylene appliances and installations, rubbish burning, chimneys and flues, ashes and soot, mechanical heat and sparks, naked lights, fireworks and spontaneous combustion. It is thought that about three per cent are malicious or intentional.

Although it is not possible to determine what proportion of fires can be attributed directly to carelessness, it is certain that a very large percentage would not have occurred if reasonable care had been exercised. It is safe to assume that nearly all of the fires caused by smoking materials, by fireworks, by children playing with matches, by hot ashes, and so on were the result of carelessness and that quite a large number included under other headings occurred either because someone was careless in the particular action which caused the fire or because at some previous time the person who should have done so had neglected to ensure that the apparatus, wiring or other cause had been safely installed.

Ignorance of the existence of a hazard often leads to outbreaks of fire. On many occasions loss of life has occurred due to persons working with flammable materials, e.g. celluloid, flammable paints and liquids, lacking the knowledge that the materials were hazardous. It is important that operatives be thoroughly instructed in the dangers associated with any materials they use or process in which they are engaged.

Spread of Fire

Once a fire has started, heat is evolved and is transmitted to other materials which, if they are combustible, will ignite and in their turn help to spread the fire. Heat may be transmitted by conduction, which is the transfer of heat from the hotter to the cooler parts of a solid material; by convection, whereby the hot products of combustion—gases, etc.—being lighter than the surrounding air, rise and heat material above the fire; and by radiation, whereby heat is radiated in all directions.

During a fire convection currents spread heat above and around the fire and at the same time material nearby is exposed to radiation from it. The rate and extent of the spread of fire is affected by the nature and disposition of the contents of the premises, the construction and layout of the building and whether the area in which the fire occurs is adequately separated from the rest of the building. The smoke copiously given off may be a greater hazard to life than the fire itself and is a great hindrance to fire fighters, sometimes making it difficult to find the fire.

Detection and Extinguishment

Although the problems of fire detection and extinguishment are rightly regarded as a subject separate from that of fire prevention, they are closely allied to it, and a few words on these matters are perhaps not out of place. It is imperative that provision should be made for early detection and extinguishment as, although once a fire has gained a hold it may so extend as to defy the efforts of fire brigades to extinguish it, yet in the majority of cases a fire can be put out with as little as a glassful of water if only the effort be made soon enough after the inception of the fire. It may be recalled that Shakespeare shrewdly observed "a little fire is quickly trodden out, which, being suffered, rivers cannot quench."

Detection. When watchmen are employed they should be supplied with tell-tale clocks, which provide a check that the men maintain their pre-arranged patrols. The value of a watchman depends entirely on his integrity; a conscientious man is of considerable value but it may fairly be said that a careless watchman is worse than none at all, as he may introduce fresh hazards, such as smoking or preparing meals. Too often a man who is unfit for any other work is employed—it may transpire subsequently that he is also unsuitable for this work! It is, of course, necessary that some method be provided of communicating quickly with the fire brigade or other help either by telephone or other suitable means. However good the watchman, he can only be in one place at a time, and there is therefore some delay, depending on the frequency of his visits and the length of his round before he can observe a fire. Automatic alarms are superior, inasmuch as every part of a premises is under observation, so to speak, at all times.

Automatic fire alarms are of varying types, but all automatically give warning of the outbreak of fire or of conditions in which an outbreak is likely. An alarm bell is fixed outside the building and the alarm is also given by electrical means to the nearest fire station, thus saving valuable time.

Sprinkler installations, which are described on page 6, give an alarm at a gong outside the premises and may also have an electrical connection to a fire station. They do not operate quite as quickly as automatic fire alarms but this is more than balanced by the fact that they immediately begin to attack the fire.

Extinguishment. It is idle to detect a fire unless the discovery is speedily followed up by efforts at extinguishing the outbreak. First-aid appliances are invaluable if used at the inception of a fire, but owing to their small capacity are useless once a fire has obtained a hold. It is necessary, therefore, that they be well distributed throughout the premises in order that prompt use may be made of them, and probably the best method of distribution is to arrange them in small groups near doorways, where they are seen every time a person enters or leaves the premises. It is essential that they be regularly inspected and when necessary refilled; an empty bucket, for example, cannot be expected to prove of any use in extinguishing a fire.

Whatever means of extinguishment are provided, the fire service should be notified immediately an outbreak is observed. If the fire can be extinguished by persons already on the premises no harm will be done, but if the fire proves to be beyond the capacity of these parties—and their appliances—invaluable time will have been saved by the early call of the fire brigade. Some of the following first-aid appliances are usually provided at industrial premises.

Buckets of water are not highly efficient, owing to the difficulty of accurately directing the contents at a fire, especially if it be above shoulder level. They have, however, the advantages that they are cheap, that everyone understands their use, and that it can be seen at a glance whether they are in good condition.

Buckets of sand may be of value for use on small fires of oils or other fires where water may not be used, but are of little utility for general purposes. Sand is liable to cause damage to machinery bearings, and the buckets might often more advantageously be filled with powdered asbestos or asbestos-graphite mixture.

Hand and stirrup pumps enable water to be applied easily and effectively to a fire. Many types, however, have the disadvantage that they cannot readily be operated by one person.

Soda-acid extinguishers eject by chemical action a jet of water, and are very good for ordinary fires such as rubbish, wood, paper, etc., as are the water (gas-expelled) type.

Foam extinguishers are very efficacious in the case of oil or spirit fires. The appliances previously described aim at extinguishing a fire by "cooling" or "striking," but the foam extinguisher by "blanketing," the fire.

Vaporizing liquid extinguishers contain halogenated hydrocarbons, e.g. carbon tetrachloride, methyl bromide, chlorobromomethane. When released, the liquids vaporize and have an inhibiting effect on the fire. They are suitable for oil, and especially for electrical fires, as the liquids are non-conductors of electricity; the risk of the operator sustaining a shock, which would be possible were other chemical extinguishers or water used, is averted. They should be used with caution in confined spaces owing to the toxic vapours given off.

Carbon dioxide and dry powder (gas expelled) extinguishers are suitable for fires involving flammable liquids, electrical apparatus, and elsewhere where a fire can be extinguished by smothering or where water would cause damage.

Hydraulic hose reels with small bore (usually 1 in.) hose and $\frac{1}{4}$ in. nozzles always connected to the water main are easily handled and ready for immediate use.

Hydrants and motor pumps require trained men for their operation and do not come within the category of first-aid appliances. It may, however, be mentioned that where hydrants are provided on each landing of a building it is a good plan to provide a "fire brigade connection" in order that in the event of a failure of the water supply motor pumps can be utilized to pump water into the rising main.

Sprinkler installations are in a category of their own, as they not only give an alarm but automatically attack a fire at its inception.

A sprinkler installation consists of a series of water pipes in which are fitted sprinkler heads, spaced at such intervals that there is no part of the building which would not be covered by water ejected as a spray from them. A sprinkler head consists of an orifice kept closed by means of a glass valve which is held in position either by a soldered strut or a glass bulb filled with spirit. On a predetermined temperature, usually 155° F. (68·3° C.), being attained, the soldered strut fuses or the bulb breaks, permitting the glass valve to fall away and water to be ejected as a spray. A fire may cause one or more sprinklers to open, but in any case the flow of water through the pipes operates a water motor which rings an alarm gong installed in a prominent position on the outside of the building. The efficiency of the sprinkler is amply demonstrated by the fact that insurance companies allow discounts up to over 50 per cent off the premium for first-class installations having suitable water supplies at adequate pressure. It must be appreciated that while the sprinkler head opens automatically on the specified temperature being attained, water will continue to flow until the supply is shut off by hand at the main stop valve. It is important, therefore, that the alarm be kept in perfect condition in order not only to give prompt warning of the fire, but so that arrangements can be made to prevent the unnecessary damage which might be caused by water being allowed to continue to flow after the fire had been extinguished. Great care must be exercised not to shut the main stop valve, which is usually situated inside the building near the alarm gong, until it is certain that the fire has been extinguished. It is also with the idea of avoiding water damage that first-aid appliances are installed, by the prompt use of which it may be possible to extinguish a small fire before the heat is sufficient to cause any sprinklers to open.

MORAL HAZARD

Moral hazard is the term used to indicate the degree of hazard involved in a proposer's personality and in his relationships with others, as distinct from that comprised in the physical features of the premises or goods he wishes to insure.

It is an axiom of fire insurance that any poor physical features can be counteracted by simply increasing the premium, but that, since it is not possible accurately to gauge the measure of the proposer's integrity, or to foretell what will be the reaction of his personality to unexpected misfortunes, the only way in which an insurance office can protect itself where there is good reason to deduce the existence of moral hazard is to decline to entertain the insurance.

The crudest form of moral hazard is the likelihood of the insured deliberately setting fire to the premises himself, with the object of making a profit by disposing of obsolete and worthless stock. Lesser degrees of moral hazard are lack of precautions or negligence in preventing a fire occurring, or in not taking active steps to extinguish it once it has started or bad relations between an employer and his employees. These are probably more common forms than that of deliberate fire raising, and, fortunately, some clue to the possession of these traits of character by the occupier can often be found in the appearance of the premises concerned.

CHAPTER II

BUILDING CONSTRUCTION—GENERAL

IT is impossible to construct an absolutely fireproof building because all materials are detrimentally affected when they are subjected to sufficient heat. Even if a material is non-combustible it will suffer in some way, for example, steelwork will distort and lose strength. There is, however, a vast difference between a structure entirely of timber and a building in which fire resisting materials are suitably used, carefully designed to avoid or reduce loss by fire.

All buildings must conform to the statutory regulations and requirements in force at the time of their erection. The regulations represent the minimum standard acceptable at the period and are mainly for the purpose of safeguarding life. For the adequate fire protection of property the planning and construction of a building must usually be of a higher order, which will not only provide better protection but will enable the owner to enjoy lower rates for the fire insurance of his building and its contents.

FIRE GRADING OF BUILDINGS

In 1946, a joint committee of the Building Research Board of the Department of Scientific and Industrial Research and of the Fire Offices Committee issued the first part of its report on the fire grading of buildings. It lays down that as the strength of a structure is designed according to the load it has to carry, so precautions against fire should be designed according to the fire hazard arising from the contents of the building and its structural character.

"Fire-load" is the term used by the committee, by analogy with structural loads, to describe "the number of British Thermal Units which could be liberated per square foot of floor area of a compartment by the combustion of the contents of the building and any combustible parts of the building itself." A fire in a building of high fire-load would be hotter and of longer duration than one in a building of low fire-load.

Grading of buildings. Elements of structure can be graded according to the period for which they resist a standard fire test and it is reasonable to think that if the elements were incorporated in a building in which the severity of a fire were equal to the fire test the elements would not fail for a similar period. The committee reached the conclusion that in a building of low fire-load a fire resistance of one hour in the elements of structure would enable the building to withstand a complete burn-out without collapse; for moderate and high fire-loads two and four hours respectively would be adequate.

Although the report was for information only, it has undoubtedly stimulated the use of constructions known to afford good fire protection, and many of the recommendations have been incorporated in building regulations.

FIRE TESTS ON BUILDING MATERIALS AND STRUCTURES

The standard tests and classifications are those of the British Standards Institution and are set out in British Standard 476. The standard is in course of revision and when completed there will be the following parts:

Part 3 External fire exposure roof tests.
Part 4 Non-combustibility test for materials.
Part 5 Ignitability test for materials.
Part 6 Fire propagation test for materials.
Part 7 Surface spread of flame test for materials.
Part 8 Fire resistance tests for elements of building construction.

Combustibility of materials, surface spread of flame and fire resistance of structures are now covered by Part 1: 1953 which will be withdrawn when Parts 4, 7 and 8 are issued, as will be Part 2: Flammability test for thin flexible materials. Other tests being studied may result in the issue of further parts.

Testing is usually carried out by the Joint Fire Research Organization of the Ministry of Technology and the Fire Offices' Committee at the Fire Research Station at Elstree.

EXTERNAL FIRE EXPOSURE ROOF TESTS

The test described in British Standard 476 : Part 3 : 1958 is not that of "fire resistance", a term which is defined on page 11. It is concerned only with the hazard of fires spreading to the roof of a building from a fire outside the building itself, and not with the effects of fire on its underside. A specimen section of a roof is exposed to a preliminary ignition test followed by exposure of the external surface to radiation and flame to ascertain (a) the time it resists penetration, i.e. glowing or flaming on the underside, (b) the spread of flame on the external surface.

The results are expressed by the letters EXT.F or EXT.S to indicate whether the specimen was tested flat or sloping, followed by a letter to signify the time of penetration, i.e. A, 1 hour. B, $\frac{1}{2}$ hour. C, less than $\frac{1}{2}$ hour. D, failure in the preliminary test. A second letter indicates the spread of flame, i.e. A, no spread.

B, not more than 21 in. C, more than 21 in. D, burns more than 5 minutes after the test flame removed or failed the preliminary test. The suffix X indicates dripping from the underside, any mechanical failure or development of holes during the test. Thus, for example: EXT.F.AA; EXT.S.BA; EXT.F.CCX.

FIRE TESTS FOR MATERIALS

Combustibility test of materials. (B.S. 476:Part 1, Section 1: 1953.) Materials used for building purposes may be tested for combustibility in the following manner. Specimens of the material are heated for 15 minutes at a temperature of 750° C. (1382° F.) in an electrically heated tubular shaped furnace, external to which is a pilot gas flame situated over an aperture in the top of the furnace. The material is classified as combustible if during the test period the specimen "(a) flames or (b) produces vapours which are ignited by the pilot flame or (c) causes the temperature of the furnace to be raised 50 centigrade degrees (90° F.) or more above 750° C. Otherwise it is considered to be 'non-combustible'."

Ignitability test for materials. (B.S. 476:Part 5:1968.) This is intended for rigid or semi-rigid building materials, primarily those in sheet or slab form. Three specimens are each exposed, under prescribed conditions, to a gas flame for 10 seconds. If any specimen flames for more than 10 seconds after removal of the test flame or if burning extends to the edge within 10 seconds the material is classified as "easily ignitable" and the performance is indicated by the letter 'X'. Otherwise, the classification is "not easily ignitable", indicated by 'P'.

Fire Propagation Test For Materials. (B.S. 476:Part 6:1968.) This part was introduced because the "Surface spread of flame test (Part 7) does not measure all the properties which are relevant for placing lining materials in the proper order for comparing their contribution to the growth of fire. Specimens are tested in an enclosed chamber heated by electric elements and gas jets impinge on the specimen. The amount and rate of heat evolved by the specimen is recorded by plotting the mean time-temperature curve for the material and the calibration curve for the test apparatus on one graph. The performance of the material can then be calculated and expressed as a numerical index, which provides a realistic assessment and offers flexibility in the use of the test results.

Surface spread of flame test for materials. (B.S. 476:Part 1, Section 1:1953—to be replaced by Part 7.) Materials which are used as wall and ceiling linings and which are combustible can be tested and classified according to the tendency for flame to spread over their surfaces. Strips of the material are exposed to heat radiated from a panel in such a manner that the temperature of the strip is 500° C. at one end and 130° C. at the other. A gas flame is brought into contact with the hotter end of the strip of material for one minute. According to the distance the flame spreads within 10 minutes the material is classified as Class 1, Surfaces of very low flame spread; Class 2, Surfaces of low flame spread; Class 3, Surfaces of medium flame spread; Class 4, Surfaces of rapid flame spread.

The test demonstrates how a material would behave in the initial stages of a fire but it must be borne in mind that, as all materials tested are combustible, in a serious fire they would burn or be consumed. The Building Regulations 1965 have an additional, higher, class "O", which requires the material to be non-combustible throughout or, under specified conditions, non-combustible on one face and combustible on the other; the spread of flame rating of the combined product not to be lower than Class 1.

FIRE RESISTANCE TESTS FOR ELEMENTS OF BUILDING CONSTRUCTION

Because a material is non-combustible it does not follow that an element of structure, e.g. a wall, constructed of the material will behave well in a fire. It may fail for other reasons, e.g. it may lose strength when heated.

Fire resistance is a term to be used with care because it is defined by British Standard; to employ it in any other way will mislead. It means "that property by virtue of which an element of structure as a whole functions satisfactorily for a specified period whilst subjected to prescribed heat influence and load". In effect this means that to be described as "fire resisting", an element, e.g. a wall, must be identical with a sample which has been tested and given a fire resistance grading under British Standard 476.

Element of structure is the term applied to components of buildings, such as walls, floors, partitions, beams, columns and doors which have a structural function or separate one part of a building from another.

Fire resistance tests of elements of structure (B.S. 476:Part 1, Section 3:1953—to be replaced by Part 8) are designed to simulate as far as possible conditions likely to occur in fires. Load-bearing members carry a load equal to that normally carried by the element. The specimens tested are full size if possible but when an element is too large for the test furnace, e.g. walls more than 10 ft × 10 ft, a representative section is tested.

The test element is subjected to the heat of a gas-fired furnace and the temperature raised in accordance with a standard time-temperature curve: 843° C. (1550° F.) is attained in 30 minutes, 927° C. (1700° F.) in 1 hour and 1204° C. (2200° F.) in 6 hours. Elements of structure are graded according to the length of time for which they satisfy all the requirements. Briefly, these are—(a) they do not collapse, (b) do not develop cracks through which flame can pass, (c) the average temperature on the surface not exposed to the heat of the furnace does not rise more than 139° C. (250° F.). This last requirement may be waived for elements such as doors, against which it is not intended that combustible material should be placed in service. The grading periods are $\frac{1}{2}$ hour, 1 hour, 2 hours, 3 hours, 4 hours and 6 hours.

BUILDING REGULATIONS

Building regulations have been developed over the centuries. The City of London has had ordinances designed to prevent the spread of fire since the Great Fire in 1666 and other local authorities had discretionary powers. In 1936, a new Public Health Act superseded previous acts and empowered local authorities to make byelaws for regulating specific matters relating to building. These byelaws remained until 1966 when they were replaced by national building regulations.

The **Building Regulations 1965** are made under the Public Health Acts 1936 and 1961 and are limited to matters of public health and safety. The regulations apply throughout England and Wales except the inner London area. The London boroughs which were within the area of the Old London County Council (replaced in 1963 by the Greater London Council, which controls a wider area) are still covered by the London Building Acts and Byelaws. Building in Scotland is controlled by the Building Standards (Scotland) Regulations 1963, made under the Buildings (Scotland) Act 1959, which is wider in scope than the English Act and includes requirements for means of escape but similarly replaces local byelaws. When references are made in this book to the Building Regulations 1965 they are intended as illustrations of principles and practice, and it must be remembered that there are parts of Great Britain to which these regulations do not apply.

Other legislation concerning buildings and fire protection includes the Factories Act 1961 and the Offices, Shops and Railway Premises Act 1963 which are intended to safeguard employees and others by the supervision of means of escape, and the provision of fire alarms and fire fighting equipment.

Building control. Building regulations are made under Acts of Parliament and they are enforced by local authorities, i.e. county boroughs, boroughs, urban and rural district authorities. Building control is exercised by the passing or rejecting of plans which must be submitted to the local authority before building is commenced. The national regulations tend to ensure that uniformity of treatment is given throughout the country and to avoid the variations which were inevitable when each local authority had its own byelaws.

Part E, Structural Fire Precautions, of the Building Regulations 1965 is more comprehensive and complex than the old byelaws. It is intended to ensure that a structure has sufficient fire resistance to prevent a major collapse which would endanger life or lead to a large scale conflagration, and to divide buildings into compartments by fire resisting enclosures in order to contain any outbreak of fire within a limited area. The requirements are expressed in terms of periods of fire resistance and do not specify any particular constructions. There are, however, "deemed-to-satisfy" provisions which describe constructions that are acceptable without the necessity for them to be tested. For example, a wall of clay, concrete or sand-lime bricks not less than 8 in. thick satisfies the requirements for a period of fire resistance of 4 hours; one of not less than 4 in. thick of 2 hours. The Minister may relax or dispense with any requirement if he considers it unreasonable in a particular case.

FIRE INSURANCE STANDARDS

The construction standards of the Fire Offices' Committee are, like the Building Regulations, consistent with the results of British Standard tests of fire resistance. It might seem, therefore, that it would be advantageous to word insurance standards in an identical way to building regulations and it would certainly be convenient if it were possible to do so; but there are difficulties. Although the purpose of each is to reduce fire hazard, they have to set about it in different ways. The building regulations apply only to buildings to be erected and require a minimum standard in the interests of public safety; they are not otherwise concerned with the preservation of the building or its contents, although in many respects they have the effect of doing so. Fire insurers are more particularly concerned with the preservation of their insured's property and their rules must apply not only to new buildings but also to buildings that already exist, built at different periods under different, usually more lenient, bylaws. There must be more than one standard in order to provide a means of differentiating between buildings according to their degree of fire protection.

It would be convenient to word the rules in terms of the periods of fire resistance required but, bearing in mind that the application of the rules is wider than that of the building regulations, there are some objections. It is important that the rules should be self-contained and easy to understand but it is certain that few members of the public, other than architects and members of the building trade, know the meaning of such terms as "a wall having a fire resistance of 4 hours" whereas they all know what is meant by "a wall not less than 9 in. thick of brickwork". There are some respects in which it may be thought that British Standard tests, which determine the fire resistance grading of elements of structure, do not go far enough to be accepted as the only criterion of the suitability of constructions for fire insurance ratings. For example, tests on walls are made on specimens 10 ft × 10 ft but the results may not apply without reservation to walls of equal thickness but of greater length and height; the tests do not include a test of resistance against mechanical damage or impact, or of the effect of water, as from firemen's hoses; nor do they provide any consideration of whether after a fire the element would need to be replaced. Although elements of structure can be tested, there is no test available for testing the junctions of one element with another. Nowadays, in "industrialized building" components are made in a factory before assembly on site. However well made the elements are, unless the method of jointing one with another is satisfactory there is a risk of structural failure and fire spread.

It must always be kept in mind that when an element is graded as of so many hours fire resistance, it means the element is capable of resisting fire *under the British Standard test conditions* for the appropriate period. This is indeed valuable for purposes of comparison but it must not be taken as meaning that in every fire the element will maintain its integrity for the stated period; consideration must also be given to factors that are not covered by the standard tests.

The Fire Offices' Committee construction rules specify materials and thicknesses, etc. instead of fire resistance periods but in many instances provide that an alternative construction which is of non-combustible materials and has a suitable fire resistance grading may be considered for acceptance in place of the specified construction.

The rules for Standard V Construction, or "Standard Construction" as it is generally called, represent the standard of construction most commonly found in this country—in some respects lower than would now be required by building regulations —and for this reason fire insurance rates are based on them. Discounts off premiums are earned by buildings that conform to the higher standards, known as Standards I, II, III and IV, while buildings that do not comply with the requirements of Standard V are designated "non-standard" and carry an additional rate.

The rules for Standard V, which is not of a fire resisting nature, and for Standard II, which is an example of a good fire resisting building, are given in the appendix on pages 155–60 and comments on them are made in chapters III, IV and V.

CHAPTER III

EXTERNAL CONSTRUCTION

THE requirements of the Building Regulations 1965 in respect of walls and all other elements of structure are expressed as periods of fire resistance and vary according to the purpose for which a building is to be used, e.g. residential, shop, factory, storage, and its height and size. They range from ½ hour to 4 hours but no separating wall, i.e. a wall or part of a wall which is common to two adjoining buildings, may have a fire resistance of less than 1 hour. Roofs and roof members are not regarded as elements of structure and the requirements for roofs are described by the letters used to designate roofs in British Standard 476 : part 3 : 1958, External fire exposure roof tests. (See p. 9.)

Fire insurance rules for all buildings, irrespective of their occupation, are described in the Fire Offices' Committee Standards of Construction I to V. The specification for Standard II, a good fire resisting building, and Standard V, which is not fire resisting, are given on pages 155–60. The following notes are on the more important materials mentioned in the rules.

WALLS

The materials used in the construction should be non-combustible. Walls should offer such resistance to a fire, occurring either inside the building or in adjoining premises, that they will not give way and, further, that it will not be necessary to spend large sums in reconditioning them afterwards.

A discrimination is made between external walls and party walls, the requirements for party walls being more rigid. This is reasonable as in the event of the failure of a party wall a fire would spread from the building in which it originated to the adjoining building, whereas the failure of an external wall would not necessarily involve any other premises.

An external wall built of the specified materials is allowed without regard to its thickness but it is not to be expected that a wall, for example, of 4½ in. thick panels will stand up to fire as well as a wall of 9 in. or greater thickness.

A party wall must be at least 9 in. thick and conform to the other stated requirements.

Brickwork provides good fire resistance. Walls may be solid or they may be cavity walls consisting of an outer and an inner leaf, each usually not less than 4 in. thick, separated by a space or cavity 2–3 in. wide and tied together by metal ties. Sometimes the leaves are of different materials, e.g. the outer leaf of brickwork and the inner leaf of concrete or autoclaved aerated concrete blocks.

Masonry. Stone walls are usually thicker than brick ones. Their fire resistance depends on the kind of stone and the method of building, but they are more liable to cracking or spalling than brick walls.

Concrete, cement concrete and reinforced concrete must conform to the definitions given in the rules.

The fire resistance of concrete depends to a great extent on the nature of the rough aggregate, i.e. the material which is mixed with the cement and sand to form the concrete. Crushed bricks, other burnt clay aggregates and limestone are superior to siliceous aggregates, which include gravel, flint and most natural stones. Coke breeze must not be used as it contains unburnt material; clinker has an injurious effect upon iron and steel.

Autoclaved aerated concrete, e.g. Celcon, Siporex, Thermalite, is a light-weight building material which does not contain the aggregates specified in the definition of concrete. In Standard V it is accepted as equivalent to concrete in roofs and external walls but not in party walls. The term applies to units in the form of blocks or reinforced slabs composed of cement, sand and pulverized fuel ash which have been cured by heat in autoclaves. Aerated concrete which has not been autoclaved is excluded.

Lignacite is an insulating building block composed of cement and pulverized wood. These blocks are not allowed in party walls.

Timber. Where the walls are constructed entirely of timber it is clear that a serious hazard exists, as all timber is combustible.

Where other materials are used in conjunction with timber, the hazard may be somewhat minimized according to the arrangement, proportions, and fire-resisting qualities of those materials, but since timber is a combustible material its presence is always a weakness. A *half-timbered* wall comprises a heavy timber framework filled in with brick; *brick nogging* is similar but uses lighter timber for the framework. In old buildings the walls may be brick on the ground floor but of wood and plaster on upper floors, or heavy timbers may have been used in brick walls for bonding purposes. Sometimes tiles are hung on the outside of a timber wall or wood and plaster frame, but although the tiles themselves are non-combustible, and might to some extent protect the timber from an external fire, this is not sufficient, as, in the event of the frame being consumed, or sufficiently weakened, the whole wall would collapse.

Corrugated iron. This is thin iron sheeting, covered with a zinc coating to prevent it rusting, and corrugated to prevent the sheets bending. It is, of course, non-combustible, but owing to its lack of substance it soon expands under the influence of heat sufficiently to tear itself away from its fixings, while if water is applied to it when red hot it crumples. It is necessary to support the sheets on a frame and in buildings intended for more than temporary use it is usual for the frame to be of metal. Although metal framing would be damaged by a fire in the building it is to be preferred to timber because it would not add fuel to the fire.

Asbestos cement sheeting. Asbestos is a finely fibrous mineral which is both non-combustible and a very poor conductor of heat. It can be mixed with cement and other ingredients to form rigid sheets usually $\frac{1}{4}$ or $\frac{3}{8}$ in. thick, which are sometimes corrugated, and used similarly to corrugated iron. They are non-combustible but have little mechanical strength, are brittle, and disintegrate easily under the effects of fire and water.

PARTY WALLS

Legally, a party wall is a wall separating adjoining buildings in different ownerships or tenancies. In fire insurance practice it is a separation between "risks," i.e. the buildings on each side of a party wall are rated independently. It follows that a party wall is considered to be a fire stop.

It will be seen from the definition under Standard V Construction on p. 159 that cavity walls (allowed as external walls under Standard V and also under Standard II) are excluded. This is not because of the effects of heat but because the mechanical strength of a cavity wall tends to be less than that of a solid one. Unprotected structural metalwork is discussed on pp. 20–22.

When a roof contains any combustible members it is desirable that the party wall shall extend through the roof to prevent a fire creeping over the top of the wall. Sometimes such a party wall is called a perfect party wall but except that it goes through the roof it is no different from any other party wall.

Defective party walls include those of insufficient thickness, i.e. less than 9 in., those which do not extend up to the roof, as in the case of adjoining buildings where the party wall is built up only to the underside of the loft, and those having unallowed openings in the walls. *Holes* of four superficial feet or less are allowed if used only for and of not more than sufficient size to admit shafts, belts, straps, ropes, and water, steam and gas pipes, but if there are many such openings the efficacy of the wall is jeopardized. *Shafts and pipes* should be bricked around closely; belt drives should have two small holes to accommodate the driving and return portions of the belt, rather than one large hole to accommodate both. Openings not exceeding 4 sq. ft. for trunks, shoots, etc. of iron or steel with an iron or steel shutter $\frac{1}{4}$ in. thick on each side of the wall opening are allowed.

Doorway openings, not exceeding 56 super ft., are permitted only if protected by double "fireproof" doors, i.e. two doors, one fitted on each side of the wall opening, the thickness of the wall apart. There are, however, circumstances, e.g. when an opening is between buildings protected by automatic sprinklers, in which a single fireproof door may be acceptable.

ROOFS

The primary object of a roof is to keep out rain and cold, and we might add fire. Roofs of fire-resisting buildings must be entirely of non-combustible materials, but for "standard" construction only the *external surface* is taken into consideration. The object evidently is little more than to prevent an external fire from entering the building since any of the allowed materials may be supported on wood boards or battens and rafters, and such roofs are always liable to the risk of collapse in a fire, owing to the wood supports being consumed.

Concrete roofs provide good fire resistance. As they are not entirely waterproof a surfacing is applied. Unless this is non-combustible there should be no air space between it and the concrete roof.

Slates and tiles are fixed on wood battens or boards and supported, as are corrugated iron and asbestos cement sheeting, on wood rafters or wood or metal trusses.

Asphalt is usually laid on concrete but it can be used on a timber deck.

Thatch. A thatched roof, consisting of successive layers of reeds or straw, lends a picturesque appearance to a house, but from a fire viewpoint it is a most hazardous roof. It is easily ignited even by sparks, especially in dry weather; once alight the fire spreads rapidly and is difficult to extinguish. "Fireproofing" is sometimes undertaken, but the effect soon wears off. Chimneys of houses with thatched roofs should be provided with spark arrestors.

Timber shingles are strips of wood, usually oak or cedar, used similarly to tiles. They are not common in this country but are freely used in America, where serious conflagrations have occurred due to flying brands from a shingle-roofed house igniting similar roofs over a wide area.

Bituminous felt consists of felt sheeting impregnated with bitumen. Types which have an asbestos or glass fibre base or which are mineral surfaced are rather less hazardous than others but all will burn readily because of the bitumen content of the felt, especially since when there are two or three layers, as is usual, each is bonded with bitumen.

The conditions in which bituminous felt is accepted as standard construction are set out in rule 3(6) on page 159. Briefly, they are that the felt shall be either effectively protected on the external surface with non-combustible material or secured to a non-combustible deck without intervening air space other than that allowed by the note.

Metal sheeting covered with bitumen, etc. It will be seen that although a coating of bitumen, etc., on the surface external to the building is permitted, such a covering on the underside is not allowed. This is because the coating is easily ignited and fire spreads rapidly across the underside of the roof; flaming drops may fall into the building and start fresh areas of fire. Some, not all, proprietory sheetings of metal with a plastics coating are acceptable.

Glass roofs are very fragile and offer little resistance to fire. Timber framework and glazing bars are easily ignited, either from inside or outside, and soon collapse into the building. A roof entirely of ordinary glass is not allowed but there may be ordinary glass roof lights in a roof otherwise of standard construction. An entire roof of wired glass (see page 38) in frames of non-combustible material is permissible.

Lantern attics and lantern lights may be regarded as roof lights raised above the level of the surrounding roof and are non-standard if the glass is in a timber framework.

Plastics skylights. Sheets of incombustible rigid plastics or of fibreglass bonded with a thermo-setting resin are allowed subject to the limitations set out in the rules. They may burn, but burning drops do not fall away. Plastics of the methacrylate group, e.g. perspex, are more hazardous because when heated they melt, and flaming drops fall into the building.

Wood louvered ventilators present similar risks to lantern lights.

Roof vents. Breaching of a roof during a fire allows heat and smoke to escape but the fresh air which enters to take their place tends to assist the fire. There are circumstances in which venting is beneficial and vents which can be opened manually by firemen when they judge it to be an advantage are useful. There are differences of opinion about vents designed to open automatically when heated.

Structural Metalwork

Modern practice more and more inclines to the use of metalwork in building construction. In many buildings steel beams are used for supporting floors and roofs, and iron or steel columns and stanchions are freely employed. In the construction of a steel framed building a steel frame, or skeleton, is first built up to carry the weight of the walls, floors, and roof. Subsequently, panels of brick, concrete, or other material are erected on the steel frame to form screen walls and the floors and roof are added. The difference between such a building, even if constructed entirely of steel and concrete, and one of reinforced concrete, must be appreciated. In reinforced concrete, steel rods, bars, etc., are set in and so combined with concrete that the whole forms one mass by which the loads and stresses are shared, whereas in steel frame construction the steel framework alone sustains all the loads and stresses, the concrete providing panels, etc., between and supported by the the steel frame. It may fairly be said that the fire-resisting qualities of buildings of steel construction depend on the protection of the metalwork, and where suitable and adequate protection is provided there is no doubt that a very high degree of fire resistance can be obtained.

The effect of heat on metal is to cause it to expand. A steel girder 30 ft. long, heated through 600° C., would increase nearly 3 in. in length, and it is clear that in a fire, such a girder, supported and fixed at both ends, would either tear itself away from its fixings or push them apart. When cooled the girder would contract, and if this occurred suddenly, as would be the case were the cause cold water from a fireman's hose, it would distort. A cast-iron column in similar circumstances would crack. In a building in the construction of which iron or steel has entered to any extent, there is not one but many metal members, and the effect of fire and water, causing some to expand while others contract, is liable to cause collapse of portions, if not the whole of the structure.

Another hazard is that at high temperature steel loses its rigidity and strength, and a girder, normally more than sufficient to carry the load imposed upon it, may, in a fire, become so weakened as to give way. At 550° C. the loss of strength is very marked.

Protection of metalwork. To obviate, or at any rate to minimize, these risks it is necessary to protect the metalwork as far as possible from the effects of heat by completely encasing it with protective material, which should be capable of withstanding the effects both of fierce heat and of water poured on it while hot without breaking away. Suitable materials for this purpose are brickwork or concrete, and, while difference of opinion exists as to their respective merits, it is probable that concrete is the most generally used by reason of its comparative ease of application.

2

Other materials used for encasing metalwork are foamed slag concrete, terra-cotta, asbestos (which may be used with cement as a spray) and proprietary slabs, most of which are composed of one of these materials and embody a device for keying or locking the slabs together.

CHAPTER IV

INTERNAL CONSTRUCTION, SIZE, AND HEIGHT

THE Building Regulations 1965 require internal elements of structure, similarly to external and separating walls, to have specified periods of fire resistance. The elements include a column or beam (other than one forming part of a roof structure only), a floor (other than the lowest floor of a building), a structure enclosing a protected shaft, e.g. stairs, a load bearing wall, a gallery and a compartment wall.

The term "compartment" means a part of a building which is separated from all other parts by walls and/or floors which have a specified fire resistance. Buildings are classified in Purpose Groups, i.e. according to their occupation, e.g. shops, factories, storage, and, in order to control the spread of fire, any building (other than a single storey building) whose size exceeds that specified for its purpose group must be divided into compartments which do not exceed the prescribed limits of cubic capacity and floor area. There is no limit to the permitted height of a building but the fire resistance required increases with the height.

Insurance standards. There are no fire insurance requirements for the internal construction of buildings conforming to Standard V. Those applicable to Standard II, a fire resisting building whose floors, columns, beams, etc. have a fire resistance grading of 2 hours, are given on pages 155–8.

FLOORS

In judging the merits or demerits of floors there are two main considerations: the materials employed in construction and the existence of floor openings. It is highly desirable that floors be constructed entirely of non-combustible materials, but if in such floors there be many unprotected openings through which a fire could spread, their efficacy is considerably reduced; in fact it might even be less than that of an unpierced solid wooden floor, which would check a fire from breaking through for, at any rate, a brief period.

Fire-resisting floors may be solid—generally concrete filler-joist or reinforced concrete—or hollow, consisting of varying types of hollow blocks surfaced with concrete. In either case there must be a substantial thickness of solid material and all floor openings must be suitably protected. In such a building each storey is usually regarded as a separate "risk" for the purpose of fire insurance rating.

Non-fire-resisting floors generally consist of wood joists supporting floorboards. Any ceiling material is attached to the underside of the joists, but where appearance is of little moment, as in factories and warehouses, the floors are not ceiled and are known as open wood-joisted floors. Wood floors, if carefully constructed of heavy joists and thick tongued and grooved floorboards, with a suitable ceiling such as plaster or asbestos board, provide some check to a fire, provided stairs and other floor openings are protected. In a prolonged fire, however, it is certain that wood floors would be destroyed and, of course, themselves add fuel to any fire.

FLOOR OPENINGS

In order to restrict to the minimum the damage caused by a fire, it is essential to confine it to the floor on which it occurs. Fire tends to spread faster vertically than horizontally, and unprotected floor openings allow flame and smoke to be carried upward from floor to floor, and burning embers to fall to floors below, thus spreading the fire throughout the building. They allow water used in extinguishing a fire on an upper floor to pour to lower floors, adding to the loss directly caused by the fire and, by forming a sort of flue into which fresh air is drawn from all parts of the building and from outside through windows and doors, increase the fierceness of a fire. An ideal arrangement would be to have no floor openings, access to the various floors being obtained by hoists and staircases in a separate block communicating with the main building only by fire proof doors, but in the majority of buildings of ordinary construction this is not practicable. Standard II (pages 155–8) specifies suitable protection of floor openings in buildings having fire resisting floors. In other buildings the protection of floor openings should be matched to the protection the floors themselves offer.

Well holes. The name is given to large openings in floors, one immediately under another; the roof over the "well" so formed is usually of glass to provide light to the lower floors. An extreme case is where each of the upper floors forms a kind of gallery around the central well, as is often found in drapery and other large stores. A fire starting on one floor is almost certain to be speedily communicated to the others.

Stairs. Unenclosed stairways allow free passage for fire and smoke and, if constructed of wood, supply fuel. An enclosure of light wood is useless, and merely provides additional fuel to the fire. In a wooden-floored (non-fire-resisting) building it can be regarded as satisfactory if the stairs and landings are enclosed by walls of brick, stone, concrete, or hollow clay blocks. Openings from the enclosure to each storey should be protected by self-closing doors, preferably of one of the types described as "Doors other than fireproof doors" on page 30. If there are windows they should be of wired glass or electro-copper glazing and limited in size.

A well-constructed enclosure of any non-combustible material, having doors to all openings, is an improvement over an unenclosed staircase.

Hoists and lift shafts present similar risks to staircases, but, owing to the lack of obstruction in the shaft, a free draught is possible and a fire might spread to several floors at the same time. Lift shafts should be enclosed similarly to stairs.

Both stairs and hoist enclosures should extend from the lowest floor up to and through the roof. It is an arguable question whether it is better to have a substantial or a fragile roof. A substantial roof, e.g. concrete, prevents the shaft acting as a flue to create a draught as long as the roof remains intact, but the smoke and heat, unable to escape, find their way into all parts of the building and retard fire-fighting, while a fragile roof of thin ordinary glass, by reason of its early breakage, permits the smoke and heat to escape, but a draught is created which intensifies the fire. In either case the damage is likely to be very much less if openings from the enclosure are protected by self-closing doors than if they are not.

Belt and rope holes. These permit fire to spread easily from floor to floor, and if many exist the safeguards provided for stairs and hoists may be nullified by the unprotected holes. If possible, belt drives should be enclosed in non-combustible material, and in the case of small drives for light machinery $\frac{1}{16}$ in. thick sheet metal provides an enclosure cheap and easily erected. It is not always practicable to enclose such drives, and in that case all that can be done is to reduce the number and size of such openings to a minimum.

Large main belt and rope races should be enclosed in brick towers, outside the main building if possible, the openings to the main building being kept as small as practicable.

Spouts, trunks, chutes, conveyors, etc., should be of iron or steel $\frac{1}{16}$ in. thick, and have a metal shutter to each floor opening.

Chases are channels cut in the walls for gas, water, etc., pipes, the front being enclosed with wood for easy access. Provided a fire stop, e.g. concrete, is inserted at each floor level, this convenient method is unobjectionable.

Other openings should be protected as the case permits, e.g. by metal or metal-covered trap doors.

CEILINGS

Various materials are used to provide ceilings to wood floors, and are more or less desirable according to their behaviour in a fire. As, however, they are always fixed to the bottom of the joists, a hollow space, the depth of the joist, is formed between the underside of the floorboards and the ceiling. Such concealed spaces collect dust and possibly oil drippings from the floor above, forming easily flammable matter, and a fire occurring there is not only difficult to locate and attack but is liable to spread and break out in remote places. An improvement can be effected by filling these objectionable spaces with "pugging" of non-combustible materials or providing fire breaks at frequent intervals.

Of materials used for ceilings, *plaster* is the most common. It is a good non-conductor of heat, and, on timber or metal laths or expanded metal nailed to the joists, forms a satisfactory ceiling, protecting to some extent the wood joists against the heat of a fire in the room below. Ceilings of *asbestos board* or *plasterboard* are nailed direct to the joists, obviating the use of laths. They are as good as a plaster ceiling, provided the joints where the sheets butt together are carefully made so that a fire cannot easily creep through.

Any ceiling of combustible material is unsatisfactory, whether it be of wood, fibreboard, millboard, textile fabric, or paper, as in addition to the hazard of the cavity behind the ceiling, the ceiling itself is easily ignited and provides fuel for a fire.

Many buildings have *roof linings* or ceilings whose purpose is to retain warmth within the building. The Thermal Insulation (Industrial Buildings) Act, 1957 and the Building Regulations 1965 require new buildings to be insulated against loss of heat. Soft fibre insulation board is freely used because it is cheap and has high heat-insulating properties. It is also readily combustible, its use enables a fire to spread rapidly, and burning fragments tend to fall amongst the contents of the building.

PARTITIONS

Partitions can be regarded as comprising all internal walls or screens dividing up a building into rooms or compartments, as distinct from external or party walls. Partitions can be of great value, inasmuch as if they are of brick, concrete or other non-combustible blocks, they will tend to confine a fire to the portion of the building in which it originated, or, at the least, will prevent it sweeping through the entire building, as might otherwise be the case. To be of such service, however, they must be of substantial thickness, extend from floor to roof, and have all openings protected with doors, which if not "fireproof" should have considerable resistance against fire. Openings for conveyors are difficult to protect but some types, e.g. roller conveyors, can have a short gap at the wall opening through which a sliding shutter can be closed. Most modern factory and warehouse buildings have few divisions, so that there are no internal obstacles to the spread of fire.

Partitions of combustible material have, from the fire viewpoint, nothing to recommend them, as not only do they fail to hinder a fire but even supply fuel for it, besides providing odd corners in which rubbish may accumulate. Wood partitions are generally of soft resinous wood, which in the course of time becomes dry and ignites easily. Sheets of mill-board, hardboard, insulation board, or other combustible material are in the same category. Any of these may be improved to some extent by covering with plaster or non-combustible sheeting, and while glass partitions in timber frames are of little use in holding up a fire they provide less fuel than those entirely of wood.

Between the desirable brick partition walls and the most undesirable timber partitions there are a large number of different forms, among the best of which are various "slab" constructions. The slabs may be of autoclaved aerated concrete or one of the proprietary fire-resisting slabs on the market, while woodwool-cement slabs, rendered on both sides with plaster, form good light partitions. Other suitable kinds consist of asbestos board or plaster-board supported on and completely covering a timber or, preferably, metal frame.

WALL LININGS

Although in most buildings the walls are covered with plaster, combustible linings are used in many, especially in damp places or where plastering would be liable to sustain damage, or in order to retain heat within the building. Matchboarding, which is a light resinous type of wood, or fibreboard is often used, and is attached to battens fixed to the wall, leaving an air space or cavity between the boarding and the wall which serves as heat and damp insulation. The risk is similar to that of combustible ceilings inasmuch as a fire spreads rapidly, is difficult to locate and extinguish, and may break out from behind the lining in a number of places simultaneously. Sometimes wood plugs to which the battens are secured are driven into flues, in which case there is a risk of the plug igniting. Vermin often make nests of flammable waste materials behind the linings. When combustible linings are fixed closely against the wall there is no air space and the risk is very much reduced.

Cases have arisen of wood linings becoming ignited due to the heat transmitted through a party wall, on the other side of which an intense fire was raging. Such a fire could easily creep through a crack in the brickwork or be conducted through metalwork in the wall; cracks in flues may, in a similar way, be unnoticed and give rise to fires.

BUILDING BOARDS

There are many manufactured sheetings which are used in place of wood for lining walls and roofs and for constructing ceilings and partitions. The composition of the boards varies considerably and British Standard Specification 476 incorporates a test by which linings can be classified according to the rate of spread of flame over their surfaces.

Fibre-boards, e.g. hardboard, insulating board, consist of compressed wood or other vegetable fibres. They are easily ignited and fire spreads rapidly over their surfaces. Fire-retardant treatments, e.g. impregnation, painting, or facing the surface with asbestos paper, may render the boards less easy to ignite; they delay the spread of a fire in its early stages only.

Plaster-boards comprise a thickness of plaster sandwiched between two sheets of heavy paper. They have some fire resistance and are much to be preferred to fibre-board.

Asbestos-boards consist of asbestos and cementing agents and are usually sold under proprietary names. All are non-combustible.

DOORS

However well constructed a wall may be, it will be useless to prevent the spread of fire if there are unprotected openings in it. Doors, and their frames, protecting wall openings should match the fire resistance of the wall in which they are fixed. The Building Regulations 1965 prescribe doors ranging from $\frac{1}{2}$ hour to 4 hours fire resistance according to the structure in which they are fitted, the doors to have automatic self-closing devices either actuated by a fusible link or without such a link. Fire insurers require doorways in party walls to be protected by double fireproof doors, i.e. two doors the thickness of the wall apart, the air space between them providing insulation for the door not exposed to a fire, and lesser protection for openings in other walls. They do not demand that self-closing devices be fitted but require that when they are fitted they shall not interfere with closing the door manually. Sometimes after a fire it has been found that doors had been left open and that fire had spread through the doorway. There may have been obstructions which had prevented their closure, the self-closing system may have been defective or perhaps no one had troubled to see that the doors were closed. Fire offices insist that fireproof doors shall be kept closed except during working hours.

Fireproof doors. No door can be proof against fire but the term is traditional and is well understood as meaning that the door has considerable, not less than 2 hours, fire resistance. The Fire Offices' Committee have three standard specifications for the construction and fixing of fireproof doors, as follows:

Iron or steel doors are made from wrought iron or steel $\frac{1}{4}$ in. thick stiffened on both sides with styles and rails of $\frac{1}{4}$ in. thick plate, 4 in. in width, dividing the door into panels. The rules provide for both sliding and hinged types but in each case the opening must not exceed 56 super. ft., nor more than 7 ft. in width nor 9 ft. in height.

These doors are sturdy and resist mechanical damage but in a fire they may get so hot as to conduct or even radiate sufficient heat to ignite combustible materials on the side remote from a fire. When double doors are fitted this is less important.

Metal-covered doors. The core of the door is made of four layers, crossed at right angles, of seasoned teak or yellow pine boards, each at least $\frac{7}{8}$ in. thick, which have been kiln dried and impregnated in, e.g. hot coal tar creosote. The core is completely covered with a casing of tinned steel sheets, which are lock jointed and not soldered, and attached to the core with screws or barbed nails, the heads of which are inside the lock joints. The limits of size are the same as for iron doors but if the opening does not exceed 35 super. ft. there need be only three layers of boards.

These doors are cumbersome and the sheet metal covering is liable to be damaged by impact. Their insulating quality is an advantage.

Steel rolling shutters are made of rolled steel slats with interlocking hinges. The size of opening is limited to 8 ft. in width and 7 ft. in height to the underside of the barrel enclosure.

Proprietary doors. Doors made to a manufacturer's own specification, having a fire resistance grading of 2 hours and approved by the Committee, are also recognized.

Fireproof lobbies. When it is considered that double fireproof doors are not sufficient protection to an opening a fireproof lobby is required. The walls must be 9 in. thick, of brickwork, masonry or concrete, built up from the foundations of the building, and the floors and roof of similar materials, 6 in. thick. The compartment projects from each side of the wall and is entered by openings protected by fireproof doors which must be 6 ft. apart.

Doors other than fireproof doors. When protection less than that of a fireproof door is needed, one of the doors listed (*b*), (*c*) or (*d*) in Standard II for the protection of openings from stair enclosures (page 156) or a "fire check" door may be suitable.

Fire Check doors. Fire check is, in fact, a reduced standard of fire resistance. To satisfy the Building Regulations 1965 for half an hour a door, when tested in accordance with B.S.476, Part 1, Section 3, must not collapse within 30 minutes but need resist the passage of flame for only 20 minutes.

FLAME RETARDANT TREATMENTS

There is no means of treating wood or textiles by which they can be rendered non-combustible. If they have been treated so that they would ignite less easily, or the rate of burning would be less than it would otherwise have been, they can be described as flame-retardant but the terms "fireproof" or fire-resisting should not be used. Many of the processes commonly used employ salts which are soluble in water and are therefore washed from fabrics when they are laundered or gradually removed from timber or fabrics exposed to the weather.

Fabrics are dipped in, or, in the case of large articles such as stage scenery, sprayed with, a solution of fire-retardant chemicals, which, when heated, give off inert gases, or melt and glaze over the surface, thus protecting it from the air.

Wood may be similarly treated or painted with a fire-retardant paint with a view to reducing its liability to ignite and of retarding the progress of a fire. Such wood is prevented from flaming, but it will decompose when subjected to heat. The most effective method of applying the solution is by impregnating in a vacuum vessel; a less efficient method is to immerse the wood in an open bath of hot solution and allow it to remain until cool.

CONCEALED SPACES

Enclosed attics, roof spaces, spaces above false ceilings and all other concealed spaces are a hazard, as dust and fluff can accumulate and woodwork becomes very dry. A fire can spread easily and rapidly without being observed, and in addition to the loss by fire, damage is unavoidably caused by firemen in their efforts to locate the seat of the fire.

RACKS, CUPBOARDS, ETC.

The metal racks now often found in industrial premises are a great improvement over wooden shelving which often aids the spread of fire. Cupboards for workmen's clothing should be constructed of sheet metal. Many fires have occurred through hot pipes being left in smokers' pockets, and others through oily waste being allowed to lie in cupboards.

Size

It is an axiom that, other things being equal, the greater the size of a building the greater the fire hazard, but the underlying reasons are seldom appreciated by the public.

In the first place there is more value at risk in a large building than in a small one of similar occupancy. Should a merchant's stock be contained in one building it could all be lost in one fire, whereas if it were distributed over a number of buildings remote from one another only a portion would be destroyed by any fire. Similarly, if a large building were suitably divided into a number of sections by fire-resisting walls and floors, a smaller value would be exposed to a fire in any section. Other reasons for regarding excessive size with disfavour are that it is more difficult to locate and fight an outbreak and the possible magnitude of a fire is greater in proportion to the size of the building; indeed there is a limit to the volume of fire with which fire fighting can satisfactorily cope.

More than a century ago Captain Shaw, then chief of the London Fire Brigade (and immortalized in the Fairy Queen's song in *Iolanthe*), said that "with a well-organized and properly equipped fire brigade, it is found that 216,000 cub. ft. is the largest cubical capacity which can be protected with reasonable hope of success after a fire has once come to a head," and in spite of the vastly improved equipment of to-day this opinion is endorsed by all authorities. The figure of 216,000 cub. ft. represents a 60 ft. cube, i.e. a building 60 ft. long, 60 ft. wide, 60 ft. high, and is the figure upon which the ordinary limit of 250,000 cub. ft. in the London Building Act is based.

When a building is of fire resisting construction, and is divided into a number of self-contained compartments by walls and floors of sufficient fire resistance to prevent the spread of fire from one compartment to another the hazard is considerably reduced, though the size of each compartment should be strictly limited. An automatic sprinkler installation reduces the risk of an outbreak of fire developing into a large fire and the view is often expressed that buildings so protected may be allowed of much greater extent than unsprinklered buildings in the same class. However, there is a limit which should not be exceeded, as occasional failures occur, such as those due to the human element, e.g. turning off sprinkler valves during repair work or during a fire, lack of appreciation of the function of apparatus or improper stacking of goods, and safety then depends on structural considerations and manual fire-fighting.

MEASURES OF SIZE

The measure of a building in cubic feet, or cubical capacity, as it is termed, is an excellent way of comparing warehouse buildings, where the quantity of goods stored, values at risk and probable extent of a fire are in direct proportion to the size, but it may not be so suitable for application to manufacturing and other risks. It might even give misleading results, as in the case of two cabinet-makers' workshops, one smaller than the other but employing more workmen. Here it is probable that the larger would be the better risk owing to possible congestion of the smaller and the fact that each workman is a source of hazard in creating more shavings and waste. What is required is a criterion of *fire size*, and it is necessary to apply to different types of risk different criteria, in order to indicate the "fire size," i.e. the values at risk, the quantity of materials on or passing through the premises, and, therefore, the probable extent of a fire.

Cubical capacity (or cubical content). This is simply the size of the building in cubic feet, and is ideal for warehouses where the probable extent and severity of a fire is proportional to the size of the building.

Superficial floor area is a similar measure to cubical capacity, but perhaps more suitable in respect of buildings of one storey only. The larger the area over which a building is spread the greater the difficulty in locating and extinguishing an outbreak of fire. Unless there are effective fire stops a fire can spread throughout the building, and damage by smoke and water also is liable to be extensive. In the past insufficient attention has been given to the fire risks of very large one-storey buildings.

Hands. This is the most common measure for factories. It indicates the amount of work done and, therefore, the approximate quantity of materials passing through the factory. In many factories, e.g. woodworkers, upholsterers, printers, flammable waste is produced and the more hands the greater is the quantity. Where fires are likely to arise by reason of the kind of work done it is obvious that the greater the number of hands the greater is the risk of a fire commencing.

In saleshops, e.g. drapers, furniture-dealers, the number of assistants is a clear indication of the amount of stock, and, in addition, each employee is regarded as a possible source of danger through his individual carelessness.

Machines. Where machines themselves are liable to cause fires or to give rise to conditions favourable to fire this measure is applicable, e.g. sawmills, where each machine adds to the amount of waste produced and is itself liable to cause an outbreak; cotton mills, where the number of spindles indicates the risk from friction and the quantity of flammable material being worked.

Benches. In cabinet-makers, woodworkers generally, and numbers of other risks, the number of benches indicates the "fire size" in much the same way as the number of hands.

HEIGHT

The hazard of height is often confused with that of size, but it is really quite a distinct hazard. A building small in floor area may nevertheless be several storeys in height, while one having many times the floor area may be of one storey only.

A one-storey building is known as a shed, and a storied building is inferior in several respects. A fire on a lower floor tends to spread upward, and even if the flames do not penetrate to the upper floors there is the probability of smoke damage. On the other hand, water used in extinguishing a fire on one of the upper floors may damage property on those lower, either by flowing through floor openings or by percolating through floors. In the event of one of the top floors being weakened by fire and giving way, additional weight is thrown on the floor below, which, too, may collapse with similar results; moreover, if the floors be of wood they add fuel to the fire.

Fire-fighting is rendered more difficult, not only by reason of the inaccessibility of upper floors, the difficulty of saving lives and salving stock, and the added danger to firemen, but by reduction in water pressure.

Fire-resisting construction obviates some of these hazards and minimizes others, but cannot altogether dispose of the objections to height. A fire-resisting shed of moderate size is the ideal building from a fire prevention viewpoint.

CHAPTER V

EXPOSURE

IN previous chapters external and internal constructional features have been examined, mainly in the light of a fire occurring inside the building, but it is necessary also to consider the possibilities of fire spreading from one building to another. The term "exposure" is capable of varying interpretations, but it is most satisfactory to use a wide definition such as "the likelihood of a building or its contents sustaining damage or becoming ignited by reason of a fire in another building or other external source."

Because heat is necessary to ignite combustible materials, protection must aim at preventing heat from reaching them. A suitable wall between the source of heat and the materials will protect them from both radiated and convected heat, from the flames and hot gases and also from flying embers. If there is no such wall the combustible material must be far enough from the fire to be out of reach of flames and hot gases and so far that the radiation from the fire is insufficient to ignite the materials.

BUILDING REGULATIONS

Before 1966, building byelaws required external walls to be constructed of materials having a high standard of fire resistance but did not limit the size of openings, e.g. windows, in the walls. Work at the Fire Research Station has shown that as the temperature of building fires is generally around 1100° to 1200° C., the intensity of radiation of such fires can be calculated and that heat is radiated only from openings in the walls. It would be possible to calculate the intensity of radiation from each window separately but this would be tedious and a short cut is possible. The walling itself reduces the overall intensity so that the radiation will be that proportion of the radiating intensity of the fire that windows bear to the total elevation of the wall. If, for example, the openings are 30 per cent of the elevation, only 30 per cent of the fire intensity will be radiated.

Heat radiation falls off with distance and, as it is known what intensity of radiation is required to ignite wood—the most common combustible material on the outside of buildings—it can be calculated what separation is necessary to prevent a fire in one building endangering another building by radiation.

The **Building Regulations 1965** have complicated provisions intended to ensure that a building will not be erected near enough to other buildings for fire to spread from it to them. If an external wall facing another building has no openings and has the fire resistance specified in the regulations it can be quite close to the other building. It must be further away if it has any "unprotected areas", i.e. (a) windows, doors or other openings, (b) any part whose fire resistance is less than that specified, (c) any combustible material more than 1/32 in. thick on the external face. The regulations contain tables of the distances required, which vary according to the percentage and disposition of unprotected areas and the purpose for which the building is used.

The distance derived from the regulations is that between a wall and the relevant boundary of the land on which the building stands, such land being deemed to include half the width of an adjoining street, canal or river. The distance is only half of the "safe" distance between buildings because a building to be erected on the opposite side of the boundary must also observe the boundary distance rules and the sum of the two distances will be the distance between the buildings.

When the design of a proposed building has too much window, etc. area to conform to the regulations the obvious course is to reduce the window area or to increase the distance from the boundary. It may however, be unpalatable or impracticable to do either and there is an alternative. The building may be divided by fire resisting walls and/or floors into "compartments", by means of which the area likely to be involved in any fire would be reduced. Each compartment may be calculated separately and, as there would be less "unprotected area" in the external wall of each compartment than in that of the whole building, the distance from other buildings may be less. This inducement to divide large buildings into fire resisting compartments is perhaps the most valuable effect of the building regulations regarding openings in external walls and spacing of buildings.

FIRE INSURANCE CONSIDERATIONS

As the Building Regulations 1965 are applied only to new constructions it will be many years before the spacing requirements have a substantial effect on our towns. Existing buildings, controlled by byelaws which ignored external wall openings, remain and exposure hazard must be considered in the light of these conditions. The Building Regulations are concerned with the spread of fire from a building to others but the fire insurer must view the position in reverse, that is the spread of fire from other buildings to the one he insures. This is more difficult because his insured has no control over buildings he does not own.

There are three main factors in the consideration of exposure hazard: 1. Constructional features. 2. Distance from other buildings. 3. Conditions existing between buildings.

CONSTRUCTIONAL FEATURES

The use of any combustible or fragile material renders a building liable to be attacked by an outbreak of fire in neighbouring premises, whether it takes the form of timber walls or gable-ends, lantern lights, roofings of combustible material, wood louver ventilators, or any other material in the external surface of the building, e.g. wooden eaves, fascia boards, which could be ignited by fire. It is obviously necessary that a building should have doors and windows, but from a fire-prevention point of view each one is a weakness as being more susceptible to fire than a brick wall. Many buildings have walls in which the total superficial window area exceeds that of the brick or stonework, and some modern buildings may almost be said to have walls of glass, so great is the window area. Such walls greatly add to the probability of a fire breaking into the building, and also permit a fire on one floor of the building to be transmitted to other floors, even though the flooring itself remains intact. A flying brand is sufficient to break glass, and radiated heat to melt it, leaving the building open to any chance ember thrown up by a fire.

Unsatisfactory party walls are another frequent cause of fire spreading from one building to another. This is not intended to include cases where there are unprotected openings in the party wall—such would be a " communication " rather than an exposure hazard—but situations where a party wall does not extend sufficiently far above the roofs on either side of it to protect combustible material in either of them from the heat and flames of a fire occurring in the other, or when combustible material is carried through, into or over the top of the wall, or the wall is not of sufficient thickness having regard to the occupation of the buildings.

Areas may be described as small open spaces surrounded by buildings. They may form a serious hazard, as the walls are weak in a fire sense, owing to the large number of windows in close proximity to the windows of other buildings. The area acts as a flue, and a fire raging in one building is easily communicated to the others; moreover, a fire may easily be transmitted *via* the area from one to other storeys of a building, even though it has fire-resisting floors. The hazard is greater as the area is smaller, owing to the windows of the several buildings being closer together, and is enhanced if there be any combustible material in the walls. Difficulty of access hampers efforts at fire extinguishment.

DISTANCE FROM OTHER BUILDINGS

Adjoining buildings. Where buildings adjoin, and are the same height, the main risk is of roof to roof exposure, and this is best combated by party walls extending a sufficient distance through the roof. Where one building is lower than the other there is a possibility of the upper part of the taller collapsing on to the roof of the lower, while if a fire occurs in the lower it attacks such windows in the upper floors of the taller as overlook its roof. Buildings adjoining at a corner may have windows in walls at right angles to each other, and such is known as diagonal window exposure.

Buildings not adjoining. The more fire resisting the construction, the fewer the openings in the walls, the better the protection of windows, e.g. by wired glass or shutters, the less hazardous the occupations, and the less the size and heights of the buildings, the closer they can, with reasonable safety, be erected. Other factors to be considered are the quality of the water supplies and the time likely to elapse before the fire service will be in attendance.

Enclosed gangways or bridges between buildings assist in spreading fire, especially if they are of combustible construction. In all cases a fire resisting door, preferably self-closing, should be fitted at each end, and no storage of any material whatever allowed in the gangway. Open gangways of non-combustible construction are unobjectionable, provided they are kept clear of materials.

Covered yards. Sometimes a yard between two buildings is covered in with a light roof of glass or corrugated iron. The exact hazard varies with the circumstances, but it is clear that there is greater risk of a fire being transmitted from one building to another through a covered yard than across an open space. The hazard is accentuated if the yard be used for storage of goods or as a standing place for vehicles.

CONDITIONS EXISTING BETWEEN BUILDINGS

Although two buildings stand some considerable distance apart, it cannot be assumed, without consideration of the conditions existing between the buildings, that there is no exposure hazard. An engineers' shop may appear to be out of risk of a saw mill thirty or forty yards away, but if the whole of the intervening space is used as a timber yard a fire in the sawmill might be transmitted *via* the timber to the engineers' shop; a similar position arises where yards are stacked up with barrels or other easily combustible matter. Another circumstance demanding attention is the slope of the ground, for a building or its contents

might sustain damage by reason of water used in the extinguishment of a fire in another building, at a higher elevation, flowing
into it. Burning oils or spirits, from, for example, an oil refinery
or a distillery, might float on the surface of the water and thus
increase the area of the fire.

METHODS OF REDUCING EXPOSURE HAZARD

Arrangement of premises. When all the buildings are in one
ownership and occupation it is often possible to avoid or reduce
exposure risk by removing a hazardous process or the storage of
hazardous goods from a situation in which they constitute an
"exposing" risk to one from which fire is not likely to spread to
the main buildings.

Fireproof shutters are similar in construction to the fireproof
doors described on pages 28–9. While any of these, if properly
constructed, provides very considerable protection to windows,
shutters in general are open to several objections. They are often
unsightly, and if closed at night a fire in the building may burn
unobserved by passers-by. If, on the other hand, they are not
closed regularly the effects of dirt and the weather may prevent
their being closed when required, or the heat from a neighbouring
fire may be so intense as to prevent access to them for this purpose.

**Wired glass or electro-copper glazing in place of ordinary
glass.** These forms of window protection, while not having
the fire resistance of a good shutter, do not suffer from the same
objections, as they are always in position to withstand a fire.

Wired glass consists of sheets of glass in which wire netting is
embedded. It withstands considerable heat, for although the glass
may crack it is held together by the wire mesh. The glass will
melt if the heat is sufficient but until then it prevents the ingress
of flames or burning debris, or, in the case of a fire in the building,
excludes fresh supplies of air which would assist the fire. The
Fire Offices Rules specify that the glass be not less than $\frac{1}{4}$ in. in
thickness, the embedded wire netting not larger than 1 in. mesh,
and that the size of each square of glass does not exceed 400
super. in., nor the whole window opening 50 super. ft. The glass
must be set in grooves secured by hard metal fastenings in frames
of hard metal bolted to the wall.

Electro-copper glazing consists of small squares of glass united
by electrically deposited copper to a frame of copper fillets. The
Fire Offices Rules specify that each square of glass must not
exceed 16 super. in., and must be at least $\frac{1}{4}$ in. thick. Each
sectional light, i.e. a number of united small squares equivalent
to one pane of glass, must not exceed 4 super. ft. nor the whole
window opening 50 super. ft. Electro-copper glazing is more

expensive than wired glass, and is used where a good appearance is desired.

Glass bricks with adequate expansion joints are thought to provide equivalent fire-resistance.

Skylights. It is possible to give to skylights some protection against flying burning debris by covering them with wire netting, but this is poor protection compared with wired glass set in a hard metal frame. The Fire Offices Rules for skylights are similar to those for windows, but, in addition, the frame must be continuous and divided by bars spaced not more than 27 in. apart. The largest skylight opening deemed capable of efficient protection is 100 super. ft. Electro-copper glazing is not approved for use in skylights, owing to its lesser mechanical strength and its liability to fall in when subjected to great heat.

Doors. Where severe exposure exists doors should be of a fire-resisting type and any glass panels of wired glass or electro-copper glazing.

DRENCHERS

Where very severe exposure exists and it is feared that the ordinary precautions mentioned, i.e. shutters or fire-resisting glazing, would prove insufficient, drenchers may provide a cure. They must not be confused with sprinklers, which are automatic, fitted *inside* a building, and designed to extinguish a fire at its inception, at the same time giving an alarm. Drenchers, which may be non-automatic, aim at preventing a fire in another building from damaging the building on which they are installed, by completely covering it *externally* with a water curtain. The drenchers are set at intervals of about 8 ft. along the apex of the roof, having special regard to skylights, and along the walls, specially placed for windows. When required, i.e. when there is danger of a fire being communicated from a neighbouring building, a stop valve is opened or, in the case of the automatic type, the sealed drencher heads open at a predetermined temperature. Clearly they can be a valuable protection, but there is a disadvantage—they require a lot of water, and if a serious fire is in progress in adjacent premises all available water may be required by the fire service to fight that fire. In such a case a building relying on drenchers might lose their protection.

CONFLAGRATION HAZARD

A conflagration is generally understood to mean a fire of such magnitude that it involves a number of buildings and is, for a time at least, beyond the control of fire brigades. Apart from the Great Fire of London in 1666 this country has been fortunate in not having suffered, in peace times, conflagrations which have consumed whole towns, but other countries have not been immune. Conflagrations are the result of accumulated exposure, generally due to the absence of structural safeguards; narrow streets; excessive height and size of buildings; a strong wind to carry flames and burning debris thrown up by a fire, and a shortage of water. The safeguards are the erection of fire-resisting buildings, wide spaces between blocks, and the supply of adequate fire-fighting appliances, personnel, and water.

ISOLATION

At the other end of the scale are buildings situated in the country, remote from any town. A fire may burn unobserved for a considerable time; it may not be possible to summon a fire brigade easily, and in any case, owing to the distance it would be necessary to travel, the brigade could not be on the spot as quickly as is desirable; also there is often uncertainty of water supplies.

HEATH FIRES

It is a frequent occurrence in hot weather for fires to start on heaths and commons, due perhaps to the sun's rays becoming focused through a broken bottle or to a glowing cigarette end or match. Such fires are often difficult to extinguish or check and buildings adjoining the common may be damaged.

CHAPTER VI

MANAGEMENT

THE first action of many a fire underwriter in reading the surveyor's report is to turn to the heading "management," and thereafter, in his mind, the whole risk is coloured according to the statement made under that heading. It is difficult to define the exact meaning of "management," but it must include the way in which the business is carried on and the condition in which the premises are maintained—the American term "good housekeeping" is perhaps more expressive. It is dependent upon and reflects the character of those controlling the business, manifesting itself in a number of ways, none of which in itself may appear vital but in the aggregate enabling a sure estimate of the quality of management to be made. The factory reflects the character of those controlling it in the same way as the conduct of the employee matches that of the employer; as the old saying has it, "like master like man."

CONDITION AND ARRANGEMENT OF PREMISES

The general appearance should be clean and tidy. Broken electric ceiling-roses or switches, defective windows, fenders missing from fireplaces or stoves, empty or missing fire-appliances, fireproof doors incapable of being shut, and, of course, any tendency to allow the structure to fall into a poor state of repair are sure signs of lax management, which suggest that other, less obvious, matters are also neglected.

Overcrowding and congestion not only lead to the occurrence of fires, but, owing to the concentration of materials, enable a fire to burn more fiercely, render it more difficult to locate and extinguish, and reduce the possibilities of salvaging stock. A well-arranged factory of suitable size enables workmen to carry on their work in comfort, thereby reducing the risks attendant upon carelessness.

Heavy machinery in a storied building should be situated on the lowest floor, to obviate the possibility of its crashing through floors which may become weakened in a fire. Efficient lubrication and systematic overhaul of all machinery are necessary.

Segregation is an application of the principle of not putting all the eggs in one basket. Processes which are known to be liable to give rise to outbreaks of fire should be carried on either in a separate building or in a portion of the premises bricked off from the remainder, any openings being fitted with fireproof doors, thus tending to confine any outbreak to the department in which it originated. Similar arrangements should be made for the storage of hazardous goods, only sufficient for one day's use being brought into the factory at a time. Even where no hazardous goods or processes are present, use can be made of fireproof doors in substantial partition walls, extending from floor to roof, to divide a premises into more or less self-contained portions. Parts used for manufacturing purposes, where fires are most likely to start, should be separated from storage portions, where fires are likely to spread and the loss to be heavy. To be effective fireproof doors must be well constructed, fitted, and maintained, and capable of being closed quickly when required; these necessities are often overlooked.

SUPERVISION OF WORKPEOPLE

Comfortable working conditions are essential—money saved on such overheads as lighting, heating, and ventilation is not economy but parsimony. Where the hands consist mainly of young boys and girls, risks arising from inexperience and carelessness arise. Where the bulk of the work is done by pieceworkers it is improbable that the employees will willingly spend time, which might be used in production, in clearing any litter they make. A good manager makes a round of the premises before locking up to see that everything is in good order.

Smoking. Innumerable fires occur through the carelessness of smokers in disposing of glowing cigarette-ends and matches. Where combustible waste is made no smoking should be permitted in the factory proper, but it is desirable that smokers be allowed to indulge at suitable times, in a suitable place, such as a mess room. If smoking is prohibited altogether there is more temptation to light up when the foreman is absent, necessitating speedy disposal of the lighted cigarette or knocking out of the pipe on his return—in such circumstances the surreptitious smoker is not likely to exercise much care that the glowing fragments do not fall amongst combustible matter. It is important that an ample number of suitable receptacles for matches, cigarette ends and ashes be provided.

PACKING MATERIALS

Owing to the differences in the nature of articles requiring the use of packing materials to protect them against damage, the materials utilized vary very considerably.

The materials commonly used include paper, cardboard, straw, havings, woodwool, plastics sheets and expanded plastics, all of which are flammable. They should be kept in special bins or compartments in order that so far as possible the packing material shall be confined to one place. Where large quantities are necessary, a good arrangement is to keep the bulk in an out-building, the bins in the packing room being replenished as required. A separate packing room should be provided, partitioned off from the remainder of the premises with non-combustible material, in order that the fragments of packing, which inevitably fall and accumulate on the floor, can easily be swept up. This should be done at intervals during the day, and, most important, before the premises are left at night, the floor sweepings being either removed from the premises or returned to the bins. Any open fires or stoves should be supplied with fine-mesh stout wire guards. Similar precautions should be observed in upholsterers' shops and other places where fibrous materials are used.

WASTE

In a well-managed factory the floors are swept clear of rubbish and of trade waste at the end of each day's work, if only for the sake of appearance and of having the premises shipshape for the next day. This is a sign of good housekeeping, to be commended even if the waste produced is non-combustible, but often enough the waste is far from harmless, especially when it is allowed to accumulate under benches or machines, in dark corners, under stairs, in cellars, and other spots not easily accessible for cleaning.

Floor-sweepings include rubbish common to all types of premises, e.g. paper, rags, matches, fragments of packing materials, etc., and, in addition, the waste produced by the particular processes carried on. Sometimes such trade waste is of value, in which case it is probable that arrangements are made for its collection and sale, but in other cases it is valueless and, indeed, involves expense in its disposal. As waste consists of small fragments it is generally easily ignited. If there is any possibility of the material being liable to spontaneous combustion it should be placed in metal bins with tight-fitting lids to exclude the air necessary for combustion and removed from the premises frequently, because the longer the waste is allowed to lie the greater is the possibility of self-ignition.

In some risks, such as mass-production cabinet-makers and upholsterers, labourers are continuously employed during the day cleaning up the floors. This can be an excellent arrangement, but there are some disadvantages. There may be times when there is difficulty in obtaining labour or, from motives of economy, insufficient sweepers may be employed.

In other factories waste is removed from machines by air current and delivered through metal trunking to a collector, which should be situated outside the building. In such premises a duct to which all floor refuse may be swept can be provided at floor level and connected to the main trunking. See Systems for the removal of vapours, dust and waste, pages 107-8.

Whatever the nature of the waste or the method of its collection it is a *sine qua non* that it should be removed from the buildings at the end of each day, in order that the premises be left clean at night. It can be packed in sacks and placed in a detached shed to await collection, or it can be burnt. If the works boiler is utilized for this purpose, care must be taken in the arrangements for storage prior to burning, but it is more satisfactory if a good incinerator be used.

Incinerators. The name "incinerator" is applied to vastly different forms of apparatus for burning waste and rubbish; from a few sheets of corrugated iron placed around a bonfire— a form which should not be tolerated—to an erection of brick or concrete with a proper firing-place and flue. The essential requirements are that burning fragments of waste cannot be emitted and that the apparatus be so situated that there is no combustible material near it.

The Building Regulations 1965 treat an incinerator similarly to a heating appliance. If the combustion chamber is between 1 and 3 cu. ft. it is a Class 1 appliance; if smaller, Class 2; if larger, High Rating. (See Chapters XII and XIII.)

Fire hazards of trade waste. Examples of the waste found in a few types of risk are given below.

Textile mills. Flammable or combustible. If soaked in vegetable or animal oil liable to spontaneous combustion.

Printers. Paper clippings are easily ignited. Oily rags or wipes used for cleaning type are contaminated with printer's ink, and are liable to spontaneous combustion. Rags or wipes soaked in oil or spirit for cleaning purposes are flammable.

Sawmills and woodworkers generally. Shavings are flammable, and all wood waste combustible. Sawdust may smoulder without being observed for very long periods; if oily, it will burn freely and may be liable to spontaneous combustion.

Boot and shoe factories. The waste is combustible and some, clicking board scrapings, liable to spontaneous combustion.

French polishers. Rags soaked in spirit polish are flammable; those soaked in oil or varnish liable to spontaneous combustion.

Almost every trade produces some hazardous forms of waste, even fish-fryer's shops—greasy paper and pan scrapings which are not only flammable but liable to spontaneous heating if the oil in which the frying is done is a drying oil. Wherever machinery is used lubrication is necessary, and oily wipes are liable to accumulate. These are easily ignited and possibly liable to spontaneous combustion; metal bins with lids should be provided for the temporary reception of the wipes prior to removal.

Ashes. These may perhaps be considered a form of waste. It is not sufficient merely to remove them from the premises and dump them in the open, where a wind may fan them into incandescence and scatter them in all directions. A proper bin or pit with a lid should be provided, either of brick or metal, situated well away from combustible material. Many fires have been caused by the deposit of ashes, either in carelessness or because they were thought to be cool, on wooden floors or in wooden receptacles; in well-managed factories ashes are usually well damped before being deposited in a safe place.

PLURAL TENURE

The great objection to buildings let off to two or more tenants is that there is no unity of control, and, as in other matters, things that should be everybody's business become nobody's business. In a well-managed factory in one occupation arrangements are made for regular removal of waste and pride is taken in keeping the premises clean and tidy, but where no one is in charge of the whole building the maintenance of safe conditions is often neglected, fire appliances are apt to deteriorate, waste is liable to accumulate in odd corners, and the tendency is for each tenant to leave the clearing up of stairs, passages, etc., to others. Of a number of tenants one may have low standards and as the strength of a chain is its weakest link, so the standard of management must be considered that of the worst tenant. Instead of lighting, heating, and power being systematically arranged, each tenant may have different forms, and the hours of starting and stopping work vary, with the consequence that the building is in use for more hours than would otherwise be the case. Where part of the premises is used as a factory and part as warehouse, there is a combination of originating risk in the factory with the likelihood of high values in the warehouse.

These objections are applicable to all buildings in plural tenure, but where different trades are carried on the risk is accentuated and, in buildings in which a large number of tenants carry on different trades (known as omnibus risks), it is impossible accurately to gauge the hazard. Some trades employ a cheap, unskilled class of labour, and the risk of carelessness is enhanced, while other trades have an unenviable reputation.

NIGHTWORK AND OVERTIME

Nightwork is defined as work at any time between 9 p.m. and 5 a.m. In some trades, e.g. glassblowers, maltings, corn mills, it is either a necessity or facilitates the processes. In many others the tendency is becoming more pronounced owing to the high cost of modern machinery, which in a short time may become obsolete owing to even more efficient machines being manufactured. Overhead charges, including upkeep of premises and depreciation of machinery, are little increased by working twenty-four hours a day and in trades in which the cost of labour does not form too large a proportion of total outgoings, goods can be produced more cheaply by adopting a two- or three-shift day.

It is sometimes asserted that nightwork, so far from being a hazard, is a safeguard against fire, inasmuch as there is always someone on the premises to observe a fire at its inception, and to extinguish it before it gains a hold. While this is to an extent true, it is in the main a fallacy. It can hardly be disputed that a working factory is a greater risk than a silent one, and when nightwork is in progress the factory may be working for three times its normal period per day with a corresponding increase in the use of lighting, heating, power, and the extended risk of fire arising from trade processes. The continuous use of machinery does not give it opportunity to cool off, thus increasing the risks of friction and overheating bearings, and repairs are apt to be more hurriedly and less efficiently done if work is being held up while the machines are out of use than if they were, in any case, to lie idle until the next day. Carelessness is thought to be more prevalent at night than in the day, and, as has been pointed out elsewhere, carelessness probably causes a larger number of fires than any other single cause. Strict supervision and regular inspection and lubrication of machinery and plant generally—in short, good management—are the only safeguards.

Overtime is a similar hazard, but with the difference that instead of a fresh shift coming on duty at regular intervals the staff consists of tired workers—and a tired man is a careless man. A point which might be urged in its favour is that overtime suggests prosperity—and a prosperous factory is usually very anxious to avoid delays in output such as would necessarily be caused by a fire.

CHAPTER VII

COMBUSTION AND SPONTANEOUS COMBUSTION

COMBUSTION (or fire) is a chemical reaction—the combination of a substance with oxygen, by reason of which heat and light are evolved. The chemical action involved in the rusting of iron is similar to that of the burning of wood—in each case the substance oxidizes (combines with oxygen); but while with iron the reaction proceeds so slowly that the energy set free in the form of heat is dissipated without being observed, in the case of wood the oxidation is so rapid that the energy liberated shows itself as flame and heat. Combustion is this active or flaming oxidation and it must be borne in mind, especially when considering spontaneous combustion, that it is indeed an active, rapid form of oxidation. The lowest temperature at which this *active* combination of a substance with the oxygen of the air takes place is known as the *ignition point*, and varies very considerably with different substances. If the temperature falls below this point, e.g. by reason of water being applied, the reaction ceases—the fire is extinguished. The commonest way of supplying the necessary heat to initiate combustion is by application of a flame, but this is not the only way. The heat may be provided by—

Conduction, e.g. woodwork touching a stove or stove pipe.

Convection, e.g. hot air and gases from a furnace.

Radiation, e.g. heat radiated from a neighbouring fire igniting doors or window-frames.

Friction, e.g. overheated bearings.

Compression, e.g. air-oil vapour in a compression ignition engine.

Lightning. See Chapter XIX.

Electric spark, e.g. arc due to short circuit or to static discharge.

Frictional spark, e.g. in rag grinding machines.

Spontaneous heating. See later pages.

In any case the substance will ignite as soon as its ignition point is reached, no matter by what means, provided there is an adequate supply of oxygen. The ignition point of a particular substance is affected by its condition and its form; if it is dry it ignites more easily than if it is damp; the finer the state of division the more easily it ignites, owing to the greater surface exposed to the air, enabling oxidation to proceed more readily. As the reaction is accompanied by the evolution of heat it is known as an exothermic one.

To initiate combustion three things are necessary—

1. A substance capable of combining with oxygen, i.e. a combustible.

2. Oxygen, generally but not necessarily from the air.

3. Heat to raise the temperature of the combustible, or some part of it, to the point where vigorous combination begins to take place.

In practice the oxygen is generally supplied from the air, which may for this purpose be considered as oxygen 21 per cent diluted with nitrogen 79 per cent, and the combustion is the more fierce as more air is supplied. For example, a dull fire in a grate may be made to burn fiercely by supplying more air by means of a pair of bellows, or the same result occurs if oxygen be supplied in any other way, e.g. certain substances, notably the chlorates and nitrates of soda and potash, include oxygen in their composition, and liberate it freely in the presence of heat. On the other hand, if the supply of oxygen be stopped the fire ceases to burn, for the reason that there is no oxygen with which the combustible can combine. Most materials will cease to burn if the oxygen content of the atmosphere is reduced below about 15 per cent, but some will burn so long as there is more than 6 per cent.

Before combustion can begin, heat is necessary to bring the combustible to the temperature at which active combination with oxygen takes place, i.e. at which it ignites. It is not generally necessary to heat the whole of the substance to this temperature, for as soon as one portion of it ignites the heat of the reaction is sufficient to raise the temperature of an adjoining portion so that it too ignites, and so on until the reaction has spread through the whole, i.e. it has oxidized or burnt.

Development of a fire. A fire in a closed room often burns quietly for a time during which it gradually heats the contents of the room to their ignition temperature. The fire then suddenly spreads over the whole room in what is called a flashover. Sometimes, although the temperature is sufficiently high, there is insufficient air, and the flashover does not occur until a door or window is opened.

SPONTANEOUS COMBUSTION

It must be remembered that whenever oxidation takes place, heat is generated and that at a certain temperature, different for different substances, oxidation proceeds so rapidly that the substance ignites, i.e. visibly burns. Generally, it is necessary to supply heat from an external source in order that the ignition temperature can be reached, but with certain substances combustion can occur without heat being supplied externally. In other words, the substance, by reason of its own properties, generates sufficient heat to bring itself to its ignition point. A familiar example is the ignition of rags soaked in linseed oil. Oxidation of the oil, commencing at ordinary temperatures, produces heat and, as any chemical reaction is accelerated by a rise in temperature, so oxidation proceeds more rapidly with another rise of temperature, and so on, until finally ignition point is reached and the rags fire. Differences of opinion exist as to the exact course of events leading up to the spontaneous ignition of different substances, but it can be accepted that, in almost all common cases, the substance is a combustible one which is brought to its ignition point by slow oxidation, the circumstances being such that heat is produced more rapidly than it can be dissipated. Where the differences arise is in the means by which oxidation commences, and these can be considered under three main headings—

1. Slow oxidation commencing at ordinary temperatures, e.g. oily waste.

2. Absorption of oxygen from the air by porous substances, e.g. coal.

3. Action of bacteria, e.g. hay.

HEATING DUE TO SLOW OXIDATION COMMENCING AT ORDINARY TEMPERATURES

This includes what, in practice, is one of the most important examples of spontaneous combustion, i.e. oily waste, because the danger is not always recognized. Oils may roughly be divided into three classes: mineral, animal, and vegetable, and, of these, mineral oil is not liable to spontaneous combustion. Most animal and vegetable oils will take up oxygen from the air, and according to the amount they will absorb so are they more or less hazardous. Some vegetable oils possess this property to such an extent that they are known as "drying oils," the word "drying" implying not that they evaporate like water but that they absorb oxygen, or oxidize, forming a skin or solid substance. They are, therefore, useful as paint and varnish vehicles, the dried skin forming a protective and decorative coating to the article painted. On account of its high drying properties, linseed is the oil most used for this purpose, and, for the same reason, it is the most hazardous.

When oil is spread over a large surface, as in painting a door, the heat incidental to oxidation is dissipated as quickly as it is generated, and does no harm. If, however, the same quantity of linseed oil is contained in a mass of porous combustible material, e.g. cotton waste, the heat cannot escape so readily, and causes the temperature of the oily mass to rise. Oxidation then proceeds more rapidly, causing another increase in temperature, and so on until the ignition point is reached and the waste fires. The process takes place without any external aid whatever, and is due solely to the oxidation of the oil, slowly at first but more quickly as the temperature rises. If the oily rags are near some source of heat, such as hot-water pipes, the danger of ignition is greatly increased, because, not only is the heat generated unable to get away, but additional heat is supplied by the hot-water pipes. On the other hand, if the heat, by some means, is dissipated as quickly as it is generated the temperature never reaches ignition point.

In the example given, linseed oil and cotton waste have been mentioned, as this is the most hazardous combination, on account of the great "drying" properties of linseed oil and the loose cellular nature of cotton waste, which traps a large amount of air, from which the oil can take up oxygen, and is, in itself, highly combustible.

Other drying oils are hempseed, cottonseed, tung, cod-liver, whale and seal oils. These, and other vegetable, animal and, particularly, fish oils, must be regarded with suspicion when in conjunction with easily combustible porous matter, such as textile waste or sawdust. Wherever such waste is liable to arise, e.g. printing works, textile mills, linoleum factories, boot factories, paint or varnish manufacturers, metal bins, with well-fitting lids, should be provided for its temporary reception, and such waste removed from the premises or burnt at the end of each day. Polishing mops left in cupboards have been known to ignite for similar reasons.

ABSORPTION OF OXYGEN FROM THE AIR BY POROUS SUBSTANCES

In this group a number of carbonaceous substances are included—coal, charcoal, lampblack.

Charcoal is prepared by heating wood without access of air. It is very porous and its commercial value is due largely to its property of absorbing large quantities of gases. When freshly prepared the pores are empty and the charcoal is capable of absorbing about ten times its own volume of air, which is thus compressed or condensed in the pores of the charcoal. Whenever a gas is compressed, heat is generated, and the heat in this case may be sufficient to induce slow oxidation of the charcoal. The oxidation generates more heat and, as the temperature rises, proceeds more rapidly until finally ignition point is reached.

When the charcoal is several days old the risk is slight, because the pores become filled with moisture and cannot absorb oxygen, but if it be "revivified" by drying out the moisture the risk again exists. If the charcoal be broken up a greater surface is exposed to the air and the danger intensified.

Lampblack is a powder used chiefly as a black pigment and is made by burning oil or fat in a poor supply of air. It is liable to spontaneous ignition for similar reasons to charcoal, but, owing to its fineness, the risk is greater. As with charcoal, it is more hazardous when freshly made or ground or if stored in large heaps. An additional hazard is that should a drying oil, even in the smallest quantity, come into contact with lampblack, oxidation is initiated rapidly and the risk of spontaneous ignition is very great.

It must not be overlooked that even in the course of its manufacture lampblack of animal or vegetable origin may become contaminated, a risk which does not exist with *carbon black or gas black* which is obtained by burning petroleum gases instead of grease or oil and which is much less hazardous.

Coal is largely carbon, and the course of events may be similar to that described under charcoal, i.e. the coal condenses oxygen on its surface and the warmth generated induces oxidation. Greater heat is thus produced and chemical changes take place in the coal, rendering oxidation easier. As the temperature rises oxidation proceeds more rapidly until ignition point is reached.

It is accepted that the softer and newer the coal the greater the absorption of oxygen and, therefore, the liability to spontaneous heating—a hard coal, e.g. anthracite, being the least liable. The smaller the individual pieces of coal the greater is the total surface exposed to air and therefore the greater the hazard—coal dust and pulverized coal are very hazardous. In high stacks the pressure tends to break up the coal forming the lower layers, and the larger the stack the more difficult it is for the heat generated to escape. It is sometimes thought that damp coal is more liable to spontaneous heating than dry coal, but there is no conclusive evidence of this, nor of the theory that coal containing pyrites (iron sulphide) is especially prone because of the liability of the pyrites to oxidize rapidly, generating heat, which may raise the temperature to the point where the coal itself oxidizes.

Precautions. Stacks should not be over 10 ft. in height (8 ft. for slack), nor should there be more than 200 tons in any stack. The coal should not be piled near a chimney or other source of heat, for the higher the temperature the more danger of oxidation. Stacks should be built up of layers 2 to 3 ft. thick, a period being allowed between the stacking of each layer to allow any heat generated to escape easily. If the coal is all in large lumps, so that there is ample ventilation, heat will be dissipated without danger; care should be taken not to break up the coal more than can be avoided, as fine coal in pockets of air between large lumps is most hazardous. Ventilating shafts are sometimes recommended, but this is a dubious expedient, as if not completely efficient this provision may produce just that dangerous state when there is sufficient air to enable oxidation to proceed rapidly, but not enough to carry away the heat produced. Sometimes efforts are made to exclude air completely by blanketing the exterior of the stack with fine coal.

Temperature testing. Hollow vertical metal tubes should be placed in the stack at intervals of, say, 20 ft., in order that a thermometer can be lowered twice a week to ascertain the temperature—the maximum is usually about 3 ft. from the bottom. If the temperature at any time exceeds 90° F. or 32° C. a daily reading should be taken, and in the event of the temperature continuing to rise it is necessary to break up the stack; once a fire has started the application of water is useless. A simpler but less satisfactory method of temperature testing is to insert a metal rod, either specially constructed with a thermometer enclosed at its end or a solid rod which the watchman can feel with his hand.

ACTION OF BACTERIA LEADING TO OXIDATION

Hay. When hay is stacked green, or in a damp condition through dew or rain, it is liable to spontaneous heating. The exact course of events is the subject of various theories, but it is generally thought that the heat produced by unripe seeds ripening or germinating, the continued respiration in the vegetable cells, and bacterial action or fermentation is responsible for raising the temperature to a point (about 150° F. or 65° C.) sufficient for chemical changes to take place in the hay, producing charring.

The carbon so formed absorbs oxygen in a similar manner to charcoal, and oxidation proceeds more and more rapidly. As soon as a free supply of oxygen is obtainable, either by the smouldering portion creeping to the outside of the rick or owing to the rick being broken open in an endeavour to cool it, the hay bursts into flames. A complete preventive measure would be to stack and keep the hay perfectly dry, but this is not always practicable. Sometimes, at the time of stacking, vertical air shafts are provided in the rick with the object of removing heat as quickly as it is generated, but it must be emphasized that imperfect ventilation is worse than useless, inasmuch as it supplies air to carry on the process of oxidation. A wise precaution is to test the temperature of the stack regularly, with either a stack thermometer or a testing rod; in the event of heating, the stack could then be broken up before a dangerous temperature was reached. Hay stacks should be small and placed well apart from one another and from buildings.

Other vegetable fibres, if damp, are liable to self-heating, but, as they do not pack so tightly and are generally tougher than hay, the risk of actual ignition is less.

Hemp, jute, and flax are the most prominent and are liable to spontaneous ignition if oily with animal or vegetable oil. Bags made of jute are used for containing nitrate of soda, and when empty are dangerous, as some of the nitrate clings to the bags and, by its readiness to supply oxygen, increases the probability of an outbreak.

Cotton, although it will heat if packed damp, does not ignite spontaneously from this cause, but if oily is the most hazardous fibre.

OTHER SUBSTANCES

Some other substances liable to spontaneous combustion are—

Metal powders, especially when damp.

Phosphorus will ignite at about 122° F. (50° C.). If exposed to air at ordinary temperatures the heat of oxidation generally raises the temperature of the phosphorus to its ignition point.

Metallic potassium decomposes water and the heat of the reaction ignites the hydrogen given off.

Metallic sodium reacts similarly with hot water.

Quicklime, when slaked, i.e. brought into contact with water, evolves sufficient heat to ignite any easily flammable materials near it, e.g. straw or sacking. The lime itself is non-combustible.

Oil soaked lagging. The spontaneous ignition of oil or hydraulic fluid which has leaked into the lagging of hot pipes is not unusual.

Chemical reactions involving ignition occur when various substances are brought together, but it is doubtful whether these can be regarded as "spontaneous" and their study is more appropriate to a textbook on chemistry than to this general survey of those commonly found substances which are liable to spontaneous ignition.

3

CHAPTER VIII

FLAMMABLE LIQUIDS, VAPOURS, AND GASES

STRICTLY speaking, a gas is a body, which, at ordinary temperature and pressure, exists only in a gaseous state, while vapours are gases given off from certain bodies when they are heated, but which, at ordinary temperature and pressure, are liquids or solids. Flammable gases include acetylene, carbon monoxide, coal gas, ethylene, hydrogen, methane; and flammable vapours the vapours of acetone, alcohols, amyl acetate, butyl acetate, benzene, carbon disulphide, ether, naphtha, petroleum spirit, paraffin, etc. The term "gas" is frequently used to include both groups. Flammable gases and vapours are those which will mix with oxygen (or air, as air can, for this purpose, be considered as 21 per cent oxygen diluted with 79 per cent nitrogen) to form an ignitable mixture. The combination is necessary, neither will burn alone.

FLAMMABLE LIQUIDS

In order to compare the relative fire hazards of flammable liquids, it is necessary to know the temperature at which they begin to give off flammable vapours, because it is not the liquid but the mixture of its vapour and air which can be ignited.

Flash point is the lowest temperature at which a liquid gives off flammable vapour in quantities sufficient to form an ignitable mixture with air. A standard method of testing must be applied; the Petroleum (Consolidation) Act, 1928, lays down the use of the Abel apparatus. The liquid to be tested is placed in a closed cup fitted with a sliding lid and the temperature is gradually raised. At each rise of one degree the lid is opened and a standard flame is applied to the opening. The lowest temperature at which a flash or slight explosion is obtained is the flash point. At higher temperatures, flammable vapours would be given off more and more freely.

A liquid having a high flash point is less hazardous than one with a low flash point because vapour is given off less readily, e.g. while it is unlikely that a liquid with a flash point of 100° F. (38° C.) will give off flammable vapours in this country unless heated, a liquid having a flash point of 50° F. (10° C.) will do so freely most of the year. Such vapours, especially if heavier than air, as in the case of petrol vapour, may drift or migrate a considerable distance before encountering a flame, or other source of ignition, where the stream of vapour may be ignited and the flame flash back until it reaches the source, at which point an explosion may occur.

The term "flash point" may mislead. It does not mean that vapour given off at this temperature necessarily ignites. It will do so only if a source of heat, such as a flame, is present (as in the testing apparatus) and then only momentarily. The importance of flash point is that it indicates the temperature at which a liquid begins to be potentially dangerous by giving off vapours in significant volume.

There are very great differences between the flash points of different liquids. The approximate flash points (various authorities give widely differing figures according to the method of testing adopted) of some of those commonly found are—

	F	C
Ether (ethyl ether)	$-49°$,	$-45°$
Petroleum spirit	$-30°$,	$-34°$
Carbon disulphide	$-22°$,	$-30°$
Acetone	$-4°$,	$-20°$
Methylated spirit	$35°$,	$2°$
White spirit	$80°-90°$,	$27°-32°$
Paraffin, kerosene	$80°-120°$,	$27°-50°$
Turpentine	$100°$,	$37°$
Fuel oil	$180°-200°$,	$82°-93°$
Lubricating oils	$350°-500°$,	$177°-260°$

FLAMMABLE GASES AND VAPOURS

The vapour from a liquid can be considered in the same way as a gas.

Ignition point. This is the temperature to which a flammable mixture, or a portion of it, must be heated before the constituents will react and continue their reaction after the source of heat has been removed. The heating may be brought about by a flame, contact with a heated surface, or by other means, but as soon as ignition point is reached, active combustion ensues. The ignition point of a liquid varies with circumstances, but is always a very much higher temperature than the flash point.

Hydrogen is typical of flammable gases. If heated to a sufficiently high temperature in contact with oxygen or air it burns with a hot, almost invisible flame, producing in its union with oxygen water in the form of steam. If a flame be applied to the mouth of a vessel filled with hydrogen, the gas burns only at the mouth, i.e. where it is in contact with air, and if a lighted taper be pushed inside the vessel it is extinguished, owing to the lack of oxygen or air with which the hydrogen can combine. If, however, hydrogen and oxygen are thoroughly mixed, in suitable proportions, combustion begins at the point where the flame is applied, and spreads wherever hydrogen and oxygen are in contact, i.e. throughout the mixture, with rapidity. Consequently there is a great development of heat, producing sudden expansion, both of the gases and of the product of their combination—steam. This sudden expansion drives back the surrounding air in all directions—this is an explosion.

Explosions. Such an explosion may occur whenever there is a mixture of two gases whose combination develops heat, but the ordinary laws of combustion apply. The temperature of a portion of the mixture must be raised, by some means, to its ignition point before combination will take place, and even then, for the combustion to continue, it is necessary that the temperature produced by the union of the gases in this portion shall be *more than sufficient* to heat adjoining portions to ignition point. If the heat produced is only just sufficient to raise the temperature of adjoining portions to ignition point, combustion will continue, but slowly, i.e. the mixture will burn but not explode, and if the heat is not sufficient to raise to ignition point the temperature of the adjoining portions, the reaction will cease altogether.

Bearing in mind that the product of hydrogen and oxygen is water, and that their proportions in a molecule of water are 2–1 by volume, it is reasonable to suppose that the most active combination (i.e. combustion) will occur when the mixture comprises two volumes of hydrogen and one of oxygen. This is true, and such a mixture is highly explosive. An excess of either gas means that some of that gas will be unable to take part in the reaction, and will therefore act as a cooling agent and slow up the reaction by preventing adjacent layers from being heated sufficiently. Thus, if the mixture comprises twelve volumes of hydrogen and one of oxygen, ten volumes of hydrogen will not be used and will slow up the action so that, instead of an explosion occurring, the mixture will burn. If a third gas, unable to take part in the reaction, be present it will have a similar effect, and this is the position when air instead of oxygen is mixed with hydrogen; the nitrogen in the air is inert, and reduces the explosive and ignition limits.

Ignition Zone. It is more convenient to consider the proportions of flammable gases mixed with air than with oxygen, and the following table gives the proportions in which various gases and vapours must be mixed with air to constitute a flammable mixture. The wider the range the greater is the likelihood of a flammable or explosive mixture being formed. The maximum effect of the ignition will be obtained when the gases are mixed in a fixed proportion, sometimes called the explosive zone (e.g.

acetylene 8–10 per cent), but on each side of this zone are mixtures which are flammable, with less violence, until outside the limits the mixtures are not flammable at ordinary temperature and pressure. It will be noticed that the proportions vary considerably with different gases. They also vary with the same gas according to temperature and pressure, and the nature and position of the source of ignition.

PERCENTAGE OF GAS OR VAPOUR IN AIR TO CONSTITUTE A FLAMMABLE MIXTURE (i.e. IGNITION ZONE)

	Lower limit	Upper limit
Acetone	2·5	13
Acetylene	3	82
Carbon disulphide . . .	1	50
Carbon monoxide . . .	13	75
Coal gas	8	23
Ether (ethyl ether) . . .	2	42
Hydrogen	6	73
Petrol vapour	1·5	6

PRECAUTIONS

Where flammable gases or vapours are liable to be present two precautions should be observed to reduce the danger to a minimum.

1. **Ample and suitable ventilation** should be provided to remove the gases, and prevent them from forming a flammable or explosive mixture with air—mechanical ventilation is almost always necessary. Many gases and vapours used in industry are heavier than air, and ventilation should, therefore, in these cases be at floor level, but where the gas is lighter than air the ventilation should be at ceiling or roof level. Hydrogen, coal gas, producer gas, acetylene, ethylene, and carbon monoxide are examples of gases lighter than air, while the vapours of acetone, ether, benzol, petrol, carbon disulphide are heavier than air.

Where vapours are produced at one point, e.g. at a rubber spreading table, a hood can be fitted and connected to metal trunking through which the vapours are drawn, often to a *solvent recovery plant*. Such a plant may contain activated charcoal, which adsorbs the vapours; they are subsequently recovered as liquids by steaming them out of the carbon and condensing them. The plant should, of course, be in a detached building and isolated from the ducting by a water trap.

2. **Prevention of ignition** of any flammable mixture formed in spite of ventilation, by removal of any possible source of ignition, e.g. naked lights or flames, stoves or ovens, electric, static, or frictional sparks, glowing tobacco, overheated bearings.

Precautions for lighting and heating are set out on pages 73–4 and for electric motors on page 122.

Damage from explosions can often be limited by the provision of relief panels, i.e. panels in walls and roofs so constructed as to be easily broken by an explosion and thus relieve the pressure on the structure itself. Buildings where very hazardous processes are carried on can advantageously be of light construction as the less an explosion is confined the less is its intensity.

USE AND STORAGE OF FLAMMABLE LIQUIDS

Wherever flammable liquids are used or stored it must be considered that flammable vapours are likely to be present and suitable precautions should be taken. As the less the liquids are exposed to the air the less they will be vaporized they should be kept in sealed metal containers when not in actual use. Sometimes it may be possible to use a non-flammable liquid, such as trichlorethylene, instead of a flammable one, or at any rate to use one which is less flammable, e.g. white spirit instead of benzene.

Fatal accidents and explosions have often occurred during the *inspection or repair of vessels* which have contained petrol or other flammable liquids. Such vessels are dangerous until every vestige of vapour and sludge has been removed; even as little as ⅛th of a cubic inch of petrol in the form of a film or sludge on the inside of a petrol tank of 1 cubic foot capacity is sufficient to produce, with air, a mixture which only requires a spark or other form of ignition to explode. It can be appreciated, therefore, why the soldering, brazing or welding of joints of "empty" tanks or their inspection by naked lights or even electric inspection lamps (which are liable to spark at contacts or provide other means of ignition) frequently cause explosions. Tanks should be thoroughly cleared of vapour by immersion in boiling water or steaming for some hours before inspection or repair. Another frequent cause of accidents is that of persons with oil-saturated clothing approaching a fire or other source of ignition. Some of the more commonly found flammable liquids are—

Acetone is used in the plastics industry and many other trades as a solvent. Flash point, $-4°$ F. ($-20°$ C.). Flammable range 2·5 to 13 per cent with air.

Alcohol is chemically the name of a class of compounds, but is often applied to one member—*ethyl alcohol*. Absolute alcohol (i.e. 100 per cent pure) has a flash point of $48°$ F. ($9°$ C.), but it is generally mixed with varying proportions of water, the effect of which is to raise the flash point, rendering it less flammable, e.g. a 50 per cent mixture has a flash point of $75°$ F. ($24°$ C.). It is used in the manufacture of alcoholic beverages; for many other purposes its place is taken by *industrial spirit* or *methylated spirits* —a mixture of ethyl alcohol and methyl alcohol, or wood spirit, with the addition of a small quantity of mineral oil to make it unpalatable (flash point 35° F. or 2° C.). *Methyl alcohol* (wood spirit) has a lower flash point than ethyl alcohol. Alcohols are largely used in the manufacture of dyes, varnishes, as fuel, and as solvents for essences, cellulose nitrate, resins, and other substances.

Carbon disulphide (bisulphide of carbon), a colourless, or pale yellow, liquid, is very volatile and flammable (flash point about —22° F. or —30° C.; flammable range 1 per cent to 50 per cent with air). As its ignition point is 220° F. (104° C.) it can be ignited by such sources of heat as a frictional spark, a steam pipe, or a hot shaft. It should be stored in cool places in airtight drums, and must not be stored in sunlight owing to the risk of the containers bursting and the released vapour igniting. It is heavier than water, with which it will not mix, and a layer of water on its surface will prevent evaporation. Used as a rubber solvent, in boot factories, in artificial silk works, and as a fumigant, it is one of the most hazardous liquids used in industry.

Ether (ethyl ether). Flash point —49° F. (—45° C.). Flammable range 2 per cent to 42 per cent with air. Colourless liquid, very volatile and flammable. Should be stored similarly to carbon disulphide. Used as an anaesthetic and as a solvent.

Mineral and rock oils (hydrocarbons) include petroleum, which is obtained from oil reservoirs beneath the earth's surface, and oils obtained by distillation from bituminous coal or shale.

Spirits (including petrol, naphtha, benzene) have varying flash points, but all below 73° F. (22·8° C.) which is the arbitrary temperature fixed by the Petroleum (Consolidation) Act, 1928, below which the products are known as petroleum spirit, and their storage controlled by the Act. At ordinary temperatures they give off flammable vapours, of which a small proportion in air is sufficient to form an easily ignitable or explosive mixture. The vapours are heavier than air, and may migrate a considerable distance, or, in the absence of a draught, may accumulate on the floor or in an inspection pit.

No petrol or other spirit should be stored in buildings unless in sealed cans, kept in special fire-resisting compartments, ventilated to the open air at ground level, and having well-fitting iron doors. A deep sill should be provided to form a pit to retain the liquid in the event of leakage. Where petrol-driven vehicles are garaged the aggregate quantity of petrol in their tanks may be considerable; tanks should not be filled inside the garage.

The best method of storing petrol is in underground tanks sunk in the earth, two or three feet below ground level, and concreted over. The tank is filled by hose connection from a tank wagon and spirit is withdrawn by means of a pump situated above the tank. The pump, filling connections, and vent pipe should be in the open air. Petrol is often used in garages for cleaning purposes—a dangerous practice—and kerosene is preferable. Often tailors, etc.. keep a small quantity of petrol in a bottle for removing grease spots, but this is not a practice to be encouraged, and, if a non-flammable solvent, e.g. carbon tetrachloride, is not used the spirit should be kept in a metal receptacle with a screw stopper and the quantity limited to, say, half a pint. The use of petrol in domestic dry-cleaning and other operations has caused many fires and fatalities. It should never be used indoors.

Paraffin or *kerosene*. The flash point varies from 73° F. to about 120° F. (23° C. to 50° C.); below 73° F. it would be petroleum spirit. It does not ignite so easily as petrol and does not give off flammable vapours at ordinary temperatures in this country. When ignited it burns fiercely, and unless in very small quantities should not be stored in buildings. A usual and satisfactory arrangement for storage at grocers' and domestic stores is to have a tank situated in the open yard, from which the oil is pumped by hand to a tap in the shop at a higher level than the top of the tank. Customers' receptacles are filled at this tap, beneath which is a sink with a waste pipe, through which surplus oil flows back to the outside tank by gravity, thus ensuring that there is no oil left in the pipe or in the building. Care must be taken that the sink is large enough to avoid the spilling of oil on to the wooden floor which, if impregnated with oil, would be flammable.

Storage inside buildings is unsatisfactory, as is the arrangement, often found, by which oil from an outside tank flows to a tap in the building by gravity, for in the event of the pipe-line fracturing, or the tap being left dripping, the whole contents of the tank could flow into the shop. Where small quantities of oil are kept in a building, arrangements should be made to avoid floors being soaked with drips, e.g. by providing at the filling place a metal tray containing sand, or by using a metal "safety cabinet" enclosing the oil tank, on top of which a hand pump is fitted over a tray from which drips return to the tank by gravity.

Tractor vaporizing Oil (T.V.O.) is frequently stored on farms. It is similar to paraffin.

White spirit. Flash point 80° to 90° F. (27° to 32° C.). Used as a substitute for turpentine in paints and as a solvent.

Lubricating oils, diesel oil, gas oil and heavy oils used as fuel oil or for use in heavy oil engines. The flash point of these oils is higher, say 150° to 500° F.(66° C. to 260° C.) and there is less risk of their ignition. Once ignited they will burn freely, and care is required in their use and storage. See Liquid Fuel, page 124.

Motor garages, and other places where large quantities of lubricating or diesel engine oils are required, are now often supplied with underground tanks, having draw-off pumps after the fashion of petrol pumps.

EXTINGUISHMENT OF OIL FIRES

Water, ordinarily applied from hoses or buckets, is useless in connection with the extinguishment of oil or spirit fires; in fact its tendency is to scatter the liquid and spread the fire. Carbon dioxide, vapourizing liquids and gas-expelled dry powders may all be used in appropriate circumstances, but the methods usually adopted are—

Foam. Foam is used to form a blanket which floats on the surface of the burning liquid, excluding air and interrupting the transfer of heat from the flame to the surface of the oil. As liquids which will mix with water, e.g. alcohols cause ordinary foams to break down, a special type of foam must be used on fires of such liquids, or dry powder could be used.

Water spray nozzles. Although water must not be applied in the form of jets, water sprays can extinguish fires in heavier oils by reducing the temperature of the oil below its fire point. The size of the drops forming the spray is important—if too small they will evaporate and if too large they will disturb the surface and intensify the fire. Fixed systems, of which the "Mulsifyre" and "Oilfyre" are examples, are adaptations of the principle of automatic sprinkler protection, but fixed piping systems can also be manually operated. Spray nozzles can also be used with hose lines.

CHAPTER IX

DUST EXPLOSIONS

Dust lying in heaps on a floor, though objectionable from an aesthetic point of view, is not generally dangerous. If, however, the dust of any carbonaceous, or other easily combustible material, be held in suspension in the air in the form of a cloud it becomes hazardous, for it is then in intimate contact with the oxygen essential for combustion; indeed the particles may absorb oxygen like a sponge. Thus, the finer the state of division the more dangerous is the dust, owing to the much greater surface exposed to the air and the longer the period during which it will remain in suspension; contact with a suitable source of heat will result in an explosion.

A mixture of dust and air is analogous to a mixture of gas and air and, as with gas explosions, the maximum effect is obtained when the proportions of dust and air are such that there is just sufficient oxygen to ensure complete combustion. As the proportions depart from these, whether there be too much or too little dust suspended in the air, so will an explosion be of less intensity, until outside certain limits the risk of explosion ceases.

The source of ignition usually must be larger than that necessary for gas-air mixtures; prolonged application of a large source of heat of moderately high temperature, e.g. a flame, is more likely to cause ignition than, say, a spark of much higher temperature, but of short duration.

The dusts most liable to explosion are carbonaceous dusts, e.g. sugar (the most hazardous), dextrine, starch, cocoa, and the explosion is due firstly to the great, practically instantaneous, increase in pressure, resulting from the heat liberated by the combustion of the dust particles and, secondly, from the copious gaseous products of their combustion. The finer the dust the more rapid is the explosion. The dusts of many plastics and of some metals are hazardous.

Frequently, a dust explosion happens in two parts—the first comprising ignition of the air-dust mixture, resulting in an explosion which, in itself not very violent, is sufficient to agitate dust lying on floors, ledges, etc., to form another dust cloud, which, ignited by the flame from the first explosion, produces the second —usually of greater intensity. Dust explosions have occurred notably in corn mills, but they have also been caused by dust from sugar, cork, coal, rubber, rags, sulphur, magnesium, aluminium, pitch, wood, and other substances.

CLASSIFICATION OF DUSTS

As a result of tests conducted by Prof. R. V. Wheeler and the Home Office Factory Department, a large number of dusts have been classified according to their hazard. Class I comprises dusts which ignite and propagate flame readily, the source of heat required for ignition being comparatively small, such, for example, as a lighted match. This class includes sugar, starch, cocoa, rice meal, cork, soya bean, wood flour, malt, grain, cellulose acetate, maize, liquorice root, tea, compound cake, flour, cornflour, chicory, briquette, pitch, ebonite, erinoid, ground cotton, spent hops, cascara sagrada, and other substances. Class II are dusts which are readily ignited, but which for the propagation of flame require a source of heat of large size and high temperature, such as an electric arc, or of long duration, such as the flame of a Bunsen burner. Class III are dusts which do not appear to be capable of propagating flame under any conditions likely to occur in a factory : (a) because they do not readily form a cloud in air ; (b) because they are contaminated with a large quantity of incombustible material ; or (c) because the material of which they are comprised does not burn rapidly enough or produces inert gas.

PRECAUTIONS

The precautions which should be taken to avoid dust explosions include those against the formation of dust clouds and those against ignition, as well as measures to limit the damage caused by an explosion.

Formation of dust clouds. Machines, trunks, and other points where dust is likely to arise should be so enclosed or arranged as to prevent the escape of dust. Dusty material should not be allowed to fall from spouts, but chutes should be provided to deliver the material gently so that a dust cloud is not formed. At points where dust is evolved in dangerous quantities exhaust draught should be provided. See systems for the removal of vapours, dust, and waste, pages 107–8.

Dust should not be allowed to collect on ledges, floors, or elsewhere, as such accumulations might be dislodged by a draught ; or a small explosion, itself causing little damage, might dislodge sufficient dust to form dust clouds, resulting in a more serious explosion. Vacuum plant should be employed to remove such dust to prevent its accumulation.

Ignition of dust clouds. No gas burners, open fires, stoves, electric luminous radiators, naked lights or other sources of ignition should be used in parts of premises in which flammable dusts are likely.

Magnetic separators (which are electric magnets so placed that material fed into a machine passes over them and any iron or steel is held back by the magnets) should be fitted to all grinding machines in order to prevent mechanical sparking. Traps should be provided for collecting stones and other foreign matter.

Electric lamps should have dust-proof fittings for, in the event of breakage of the lamp, dust clouds might be ignited at the still glowing filament. Moreover, dust which settled on the lamp might be ignited even without breakage by the heat of the lamp. The possibility of arcs, due to short circuits or other causes, should be reduced by enclosing all wiring in earthed continuous screwed metal conduits. Where a flexible lead is essential tough rubber-covered cable should be used and the lamp and wall fittings should be of the certified flameproof type. Switches, starters, fuses, motors, etc., should be of the flameproof type or be remotely placed in dust-free situations.

Static electricity is likely to be generated, but the likelihood of spark discharges can be minimized by suitably earthing machines, pulleys, etc., or, better, where the nature of the material being used permits, by humidifying the air, as this is not only a safeguard against static discharges, but reduces the flammability of the dust.

Where, as for example in coal mines, sufficient non-combustible dust, e.g. stone dust, can be added to a material an explosion may be prevented and, in some instances, it may be possible to utilize inert gas in a similar manner.

Limiting explosion damage. The more confined an explosion, the greater is its intensity. By the provision of light relief panels in grinding machines, elevators, etc., the expanding gases are enabled to escape more easily. An explosion in a machine can often be prevented from passing to other plant fed by it by interposing a worm conveyor choke tube or a rotary valve. As far as possible grinding machines should be installed in separate fire-resisting rooms having adequate relief panels.

Specially hazardous materials. The grinding of cork, dyestuffs, aluminium, and magnesium and its alloys, is especially hazardous and special precautions are necessary. Water or chemical extinguishers must not be used where metallic dusts are ground—powdered asbestos, asbestos graphite, powdered talc or dry sand should be applied gently so as not to disturb the dust.

CHAPTER X

CELLULOID—PAINT SPRAYING

CELLULOSE is the chief component of all vegetable tissues, in which it exists as cells or fibres. Cotton-wool is almost pure cellulose and, for this reason, is the form most used in manufacturing cellulose products.

By treating purified cotton-wool with nitric and sulphuric acids, nitro-cellulose is produced, the characteristics of which vary according to the proportion of nitrogen in it. Gun-cotton is both combustible and explosive, but the more important product commercially is cellulose nitrate (or nitro-cellulose) in which the nitration has not been carried so far as in gun-cotton, i.e. its proportion of nitrogen is less. Although not explosive, it is so highly flammable that its combustion may, in favourable circumstances, almost appear to be an explosion, and it can continue to burn in the absence of air. It is soluble in alcohol and some other solvents, and is used in the manufacture of celluloid, and cellulose paints and varnishes.

CELLULOID

Celluloid, also known as xylonite or pyroxylin plastic, is a mixture of cellulose nitrate and camphor dissolved in ether and alcohol or other solvents. The solvent is dried out, leaving celluloid, a tough, hard material which is used in the manufacture of some toys, imitation tortoiseshell, fancy articles, etc. It is highly flammable, is easily ignited, and burns rapidly and fiercely. If heated to a temperature of 250°–300° F. (121°–149° C.) without the application of flame (as might happen if celluloid were stored against steam or even high pressure hot-water pipes) it decomposes rapidly, giving off a flammable and poisonous vapour. Should this vapour be mixed with the correct proportion of air and ignited, an explosion would result.

Celluloid articles have been known to ignite owing to their being in contact with incandescent electric-light bulbs, due to the soldering of tins and the use of sealing wax on packages containing celluloid, and by friction as in cutting with a saw (this should be done under a jet of water). Owing to its large percentage of oxygen it will continue to burn in the absence of air, and for this reason it is practically impossible to extinguish fires in large quantities of celluloid. Copious quantities of water should be applied for cooling purposes.

Wherever celluloid is worked or used the amount in the workshop should be restricted to a minimum by bringing in, at a time, only sufficient for immediate needs, and removing as soon as possible. All scraps and cuttings should be collected in self-closing metal bins and removed frequently. There should be no open lights, fires or other means of ignition and smoking should be prohibited. Where celluloid articles are stored they should be kept in closed metal cases, and if there is more than 1 cwt. the stock should be kept in compartments of fire-resisting construction.

Cinematograph film. At one time all cinematograph film had a cellulose nitrate (celluloid) base. Such film, still kept perhaps for record purposes, is especially flammable, and should be stored in well ventilated fire-resisting vaults, strictly limited as to size. Each spool should be in a separate metal container, and a space should be allowed between containers, in order to prevent the heat of a fire in one from being conducted to the others. Cinematograph film is now made of cellulose acetate, and such stringent precautions are not required, but as cellulose acetate lacks some of the qualities of cellulose nitrate it is possible that "acetate" film may include a proportion of cellulose nitrate, either as a mixture or in the form of a coating on a cellulose acetate base. In either event, the proportion is small.

"Safety" film base is usually made from cellulose acetate (i.e. the cellulose is treated with acetic acid instead of nitric acid) and burns in the manner of paper rather than the fierce and rapid way of celluloid. It is used for making photographic films, transparent wrapping papers, e.g. cellophane, etc. Many articles previously moulded from celluloid are now moulded in nonflammable plastics, e.g. erinoid, bakelite, etc.

CELLULOSE SOLUTIONS (PAINTS, LACQUERS, VARNISHES, ETC.)

The simplest form of cellulose solution would be scrap celluloid dissolved in, say, acetone, and if such a solution were applied to a surface the solvent would evaporate, leaving a thin coating or film of celluloid on the surface. During the evaporation of the solvent the vapour would mix with the air and, if in suitable proportions, form a flammable mixture which could be ignited by a spark, flame, or other source of ignition.

At one time, scrap celluloid and stripped cinematograph film were indeed used, but nowadays almost all cellulose solutions have, as a basis, cellulose nitrate dissolved in a suitable solvent. The solvents commonly used include amyl acetate, butyl acetate, ethyl acetate, acetone and alcohols, and the solution is diluted with methylated spirit, benzene, methyl alcohol and other liquids having low flash points. Such a solution would, on drying, leave a somewhat brittle film, and flexibility is given by "plasticizers" in the form of castor-oil, gums, and resins. Pigments to give the desired colour to the solution are added. The user thins the solutions to the desired consistency by the use of "thinners," which, too, are flammable liquids with low flash points.

Originally such solutions were used in the manufacture of waterproof cloths and imitation leathers, being applied to textile fabrics in more or less airtight machines, but nowadays cellulose painting is practised in many trades.

CELLULOSE-PAINT SPRAYING

Articles are sometimes dipped in baths of cellulose paint or the paint may be applied by brush or they may be "flow-coated" by a stream of paint flowing over them; but the usual method of application is by spraying. The advantage of this method is that it is very much quicker both in application and drying than ordinary brush-painting, and, in skilled hands, gives a very good appearance to the work.

The spraying is done by means of apparatus consisting of a receptacle in which paint is placed, and from which it flows in a thin stream to a "pistol," where it is met by a stream of compressed air, fed to the pistol through a flexible tube, from an air compressor. The air pressure breaks up the paint stream to a fine spray, which is projected on to the article to be painted; though a quantity is inadvertently sprayed on the surroundings, such as the bench or floor on which the article is placed. These deposits, being essentially cellulose nitrate, are exceedingly flammable, and it is necessary that they are not allowed to accumulate. A fibre or non-ferrous scraper should be used to remove them, as, if an iron instrument were used, a frictional spark might ignite either the scrapings or any dust from them in the surrounding air. They are liable to spontaneous combustion, especially if allowed to accumulate on a heated surface, e.g. steam pipes, or if cellulose paints are sprayed alternately with oil paints.

When cellulose paints dry they do not, as in the case of oil paints, slowly oxidize, but the solvents simply evaporate, leaving behind the solid constituents as a film. The vapours thus given off are both harmful to health and form explosive mixtures with air. These vapours may be considered in the same way as any other flammable vapour, and the precautions to be observed fall into two groups—ventilation to remove the vapours as quickly as they are formed, and exclusion of any possible source of ignition. Small articles are sprayed in cabinets or booths enclosed on all sides except the front, where the operator stands, and ventilated at the back by a fan. Generally, several of these booths are erected against an external wall in order that the fans may exhaust direct to the open air. Large articles, such as motor-cars, require to be painted in separate rooms, and no work other than spraying should be allowed in these.

Electro-static spraying. Paint is charged to a high voltage as it is sprayed from either fixed nozzles or a hand held gun and the article being painted is earthed. Electrostatic forces attract the paint droplets to the article.

PRECAUTIONS

Situation. All handling of cellulose solutions, whether mixing, spraying, or other process, should take place only in a compartment used for no other purpose, separated from the remainder of the premises by walls or partitions of, or lined with, non-combustible materials, so constructed as to prevent vapours drifting to other departments. Unless the partitions extend to the ceiling or roof a false ceiling should be provided. Doors if not of metal or hard-wood should be lined with non-combustible material and should be self-closing. Glazing in doors or partitions should be of wired glass.

Ventilation. Artificial exhaust ventilation is always necessary, the heaviness of the vapours precluding reliance being placed on natural ventilation. Whenever possible the fans should discharge direct to the open air, but where this cannot be arranged the ducts should be of large diameter, constructed of metal, as short as practicable and without sharp bends in order to avoid accumulations of residues. Sometimes water sprays are provided through which the exhaust vapours pass and by which a large proportion of the residue is trapped.

The exhaust fans, which should be at or near floor level, should provide an air velocity of at least 100 linear feet per minute at the working opening and should be run for at least five minutes after work has ceased. They should be driven either by flameproof electric motors or by belt from a motor or other source of power outside the compartment and ventilating duct.

Booths which are not in such a compartment should be built of metal and wired glass, situated against an external wall and ventilated by a fan discharging to the open.

Deposits or residues are readily flammable and may be ignited by a frictional spark. They are also liable to spontaneous combustion. Booths, ducts and elsewhere where deposits can accumulate should be cleaned frequently, at least weekly, with brushes or scrapers of non-sparking material and the scrapings placed in metal receptacles, wetted and removed immediately. Used cleaning rags, etc., should be kept in metal bins and removed daily.

Lighting. The only suitable form of artificial lighting is electricity, filament lamps being in well glass or bulkhead fittings, and fluorescent lamps, including chokes, etc., in flameproof fittings. Where electricity is not available gas or other lighting may be installed externally, the light entering the compartment through windows or skylights of fixed plate glass.

Heating. Acceptable methods of heating comprise electric heaters of the totally enclosed type provided the external surface does not exceed $180°$ F. ($82 \cdot 2°$ C.), low-pressure hot water, steam at a gauge pressure of not more that 10 lb. per sq. in. or hot air through metal ducts from hot water, steam or electric heaters; the boiler in each case being outside the compartment. Ovens or other drying appliances are not permissible unless similarly heated. Ordinary glowing element electric fires, gas fires or radiators or any other forms of heating must not be used. Smoking should be prohibited in or near the room.

Electrical equipment should, as far as possible, be excluded from the compartment, and all necessary apparatus should conform to the Regulations of the Institution of Electrical Engineers. Wiring should be in metal conduit screwed at the ends into the cases or fittings, etc., so as to enclose completely the whole length of the wiring. Motors, switches, and all other apparatus and fittings should be of the flameproof type, and no portable appliances or flexible wiring used. Fuses and any non-flameproof equipment should be outside the compartment.

Storage. The stocks of paint, thinners, etc., should be kept in a detached store of fire-resisting construction provided with a deep sill in order that any leakage shall be retained. Only sufficient for one day's use should be taken into the workshop, and while there should be kept in a locked metal bin when not in actual use. Empty drums and tins should be removed to the storeroom.

Extinguishment. The provision of ample fire-extinguishing appliances is very desirable. Some doubt has been cast on the efficacy of foam extinguishers, as cellulose solvents and thinners tend to break down the foam bubbles. It has, however, been demonstrated that some types of foam are satisfactory and that much depends on the rate of application. It is probable that this type of extinguisher is generally the most suitable.

SPRAYING OF OTHER THAN NITRO-CELLULOSE SOLUTIONS

Although nitro-cellulose solutions are those most commonly used, almost any liquid or semi-liquid can be sprayed. Synthetic paints, i.e. those embodying synthetic resins are widely regarded as much safer than cellulose paints. It is true that deposits from these paints are less hazardous than cellulose deposits, but the solvents used are similar, and flammable vapours are freely given off, as is also the case with aluminium paint. The fire offices' recommendations apply not only to cellulose paints but to the application either by spraying or by other means of any flammable liquid, i.e. paint, varnish, lacquer, enamel, polish or similar material which has a flash point of less than 73° F. (22·8° C.), or of less than 90° F. (32·2° C.) where the liquid is used or intended for use in connection with a cellulose solution.

In the building and decorating trades ordinary oil paints, varnishes, and emulsions are applied. In the furniture and leather trades, french polish and various water or spirit stains are frequently sprayed, and in many other trades spraying finds application. The risk varies according to the properties of the materials and the solvents employed, bearing in mind that, if combustible in their usual condition, they will be more easily combustible when mixed with air in the form of a spray. Any of those usually employed is less hazardous than a nitro-cellulose solution, and the precautions may be relaxed to a greater or lesser extent according to the hazard of the constituents, particularly of the solvents used as indicated by their flash points. Where the degree of hazard is not clear, information can often be obtained from the manufacturers as to the composition of the preparation.

Paint Dipping Tanks

When articles are dipped into tanks of paint, rust-proofing solutions, or other combustible liquids the hazard depends on the flammability of the liquid and the quantity in use. Small tanks should be fitted with close-fitting lids which can be quickly closed, either manually or by the operation of a fusible link in a wire which normally holds the lid open. This form of protection cannot be applied to large tanks or where obstructions would prevent the lid closing. Continuous dipping and drying plants, such as are used by motor-car manufacturers, where the dipping tank is followed by a drying tunnel or oven, are often protected by an automatic carbon dioxide extinguishing system.

CHAPTER XI

LIGHTING AND HEATING—GENERAL

IN any classification of the causes of fire it is found that a substantial proportion is attributed to forms of lighting and heating. That "heating" figures prominently should not cause any surprise, as a fire in, say, a grate is of the same nature as a fire which demands the attention of the Fire Service; the only difference, although this is an important one, being that the first is confined to its proper place, while the second is, as it were, unfettered. Light in itself is not a hazard, but as in all forms of lighting heat is occasioned, lighting can well be considered, from the point of view of fire hazard, as a form of heating.

From the humblest cottage to the largest factory the risks of fire arising from lighting and heating systems exist, and whatever the method employed its hazards should be considered under two headings: (1) The hazard inherent in the method, which, of course, cannot be entirely eliminated, although it can be minimized; (2) the particular risks due to the situation where the apparatus is installed, including the conditions under which it is used. As an example, lighting by coal gas usually presents quite a small hazard, but if a gas burner is installed in a cellulose spraying booth, the likelihood of a fire occurring is very great. A fire-heated stove may be non-hazardous standing on a concrete floor in an engineer's workshop, but it is a real hazard on a wooden floor in a saw mill.

FLAME

In all forms of lighting other than by electricity a flame is utilized, either as a luminous flame by itself, e.g. a candle, or in the form of a non-luminous flame employed to heat a mantle to incandescence. Flame may be said to be burning gas, e.g. when coal gas burns a chemical action takes place in which the combination of hydrogen, oxygen, and carbon generates heat. If this combination, or combustion, is imperfect, minute particles of carbon in the centre of the flame, which are not in contact with air and are unable to enter into combination, become heated to incandescence by the heat of the reaction of the oxygen and hydrogen, and thus a luminous flame is produced. If, however, sufficient air is mixed with the coal gas before it enters the burner, these carbon particles are in contact with oxygen and are able to enter into combination with it. This enables more perfect combustion to take place, and although light is not emitted, more heat is generated. It may be said then that a non-luminous flame is hotter than a luminous one, and such a flame is employed to heat to incandescence a mantle which, being impregnated with substances which emit a brighter light than carbon particles, gives a stronger light than a luminous flame by itself.

It is well to remember that all ordinary flames are burning gas. Although liquids and solids appear to produce flames when they burn, the flame is in fact the burning of the vapours and gases to which heat has converted the liquids and solids. This can be seen clearly by close examination of the flame of a candle or a lighted match.

FIRE HAZARDS

There are a number of hazards common to most forms of lighting and heating.

Naked flames. Wherever there is an unprotected flame, the possibility exists of combustible material coming into contact with it. Many fires are caused by materials coming into contact with an open fire or a glowing electric element.

Fireguards provide considerable protection. Open coal or coke fires should be fitted with a wire guard so designed that the fire can be refuelled and ashes can be withdrawn without removing the guard. A guard having eight meshes to the inch serves also as a spark guard.

Regulations under the Heating Appliances (Fireguards) Act, 1952, require that appropriate guards shall be fitted to gas fires, electric fires, and oil-burning heaters of types suitable for use in dwellings if, without a guard, there would be a likelihood of injury by burning.

Portable appliances. When any lighting or heating appliance is movable the hazard is increased, because not only can combustible material be placed in contact with the appliance, but the appliance can be moved into contact with combustible material; it can also be knocked over.

Effect of heat on combustible materials. The fact that flammable material, such as textile fabrics, coming into contact with naked flames is likely to start a fire, is generally understood, but it is not so commonly appreciated that heat alone (without any flame) will ignite such articles. Clothes left airing in front of and too near to an open coal or gas fire often ignite because sparks are thrown on to them or they fall into the fire, but they are also often ignited merely by the radiated heat, which first scorches the clothes and then causes them to ignite. Electric lamps have been known to become hot enough to ignite combustible matter in contact with them, especially if the lamps are so enclosed that the heat is unable to get away.

As wood is used to such a large extent in the internal construction and furnishing of buildings it is important that the effect of heat on wood is understood. Up to about 100° C. or 212° F. only the moisture which is contained in the pores of the wood is driven out, but at slightly higher temperatures minor changes occur. At about 149° C. or 300° F. flammable gases begin to be expelled; at about 232° C. or 450° F. the wood commences to change into a form of charcoal; at about 274° C. or 525° F. it decomposes rapidly and will ignite in the presence of a small flame; at higher temperatures it will ignite spontaneously.

In a fire, the combustion first takes the form of flaming of the gases; subsequently the non-volatile charcoal-like remains glow and produce the combustible gas, carbon monoxide.

Timber should not be subjected to continuous heating at temperatures over 100° C. (212° F.). The most effective precaution is to arrange that no wood is sufficiently near to any form of heat to be endangered in this manner. The distance which should be observed depends on the nature of the heating or lighting apparatus involved and also whether the wood is over, under, or at the side of the source of heat. The summaries of building regulations on pages 80–2 and 89–90 indicate suitable safeguards. In other circumstances, when the heat is not too great, some protection can be given to woodwork by fixing metal or asbestos cement sheeting between the source of heat and the woodwork. The sheeting must not be in contact with the wood, but can be satisfactorily secured to it by long screws having distance pieces so that the metal is, at least, 1 in. from the wood, thus permitting a current of air, itself a good heat insulator, to circulate between the sheet and the woodwork.

Lighting up. Most lighting and heating devices, with the exception of electric ones, require to be lit by means of a spark or flame. If matches are used, the still glowing match may be carelessly thrown down and ignite some flammable material, or, if a piece of paper or a wax or wooden spill is used to transfer a flame from one point to another, it is possible for burning fragments to fall from it. It is not unknown for paper so used to burn the fingers of the "lighter up" who promptly drops the still flaming torch. But note: smokers, too, use matches and spills. For lighting gas-burning appliances an electric lighter is a suitable instrument.

Flammable gases, vapours, and dusts. In places where flammable gases, vapours, or dusts are likely to be present it is essential that the methods of lighting and heating adopted are not such as would provide a source of ignition.

The only permissible form of lighting in such a building is electric, and the lamps or tubes should be enclosed in flameproof fittings (see page 100). All wiring should be completely enclosed in earthed continuous metal conduit screwed at both ends into the cases of fittings, etc. Inspection lamps with trailing leads and other portable apparatus should not be used. Switches, if not flameproof, and fuses should be remotely placed in vapour-free situations. If electricity is not available gas or other lights should be installed externally, the light entering the building or room through windows of fixed plate glass.

The most suitable methods of heating are low-pressure steam or hot-water pipes or radiators, or hot air through metal ducts, the boiler or other heating apparatus in each case being outside the building in a vapour-free situation. Where concentrations of vapour, etc., may occur but are not likely to be continuous or heavy, some relaxation, appropriate to the circumstances, may be made. For example, in motor garages, petrol vapour, which is heavier than air, is only likely when petrol has been spilled or has escaped from containers. No objection is usually taken to gas or electric appliances fixed more than 6 feet above ground level, gas radiators of the "garage type" described on page 85, or oil-fired space heaters (see page 77) if the air intake to the burners is at least 6 feet above ground level or direct from the open, the products of combustion are discharged direct to the open, and the arrangements for oil storage and supply are satisfactory. Ordinary gas or electric fires, open fires, pipe stoves, and any other appliance which might provide a source of ignition to the gas, vapour or dust should not be permitted, nor should portable apparatus be used.

BUILDING REGULATIONS

The installation of heat-producing appliances (including cookers) which burn solid fuel, oil or gas is controlled by the Building Regulations 1965 but appliances consuming electricity do not come within the regulations.

Class I appliances are those which burn solid fuel or oil. The provisions apply also to solid fuel fires which burn directly on a hearth without any appliance (see Chapter XII).

Class II appliances are those which burn gas (see Chapter XIII).

It must be borne in mind that the regulations apply only to new installations and that many existing installations are of a lower standard.

LIGHTING AND HEATING BY OIL AND SOLID FUELS

THE appliances considered in this chapter are those which are individually installed in the area or space to be heated. Central heating installations, which heat a building by means of a system of pipes carrying steam, hot water or air from a central boiler or furnace, are described in Chapter XV. The precautions to be taken are outlined under "Building Regulations" on pages 80–2. Where the regulations do not apply, i.e. to installations before 1966, they provide reliable guidance.

LIGHTING AND HEATING BY OIL

There is a wide variety of oil-burning appliances, both fixed and portable. Those described in this chapter burn kerosene (paraffin) or light oils having flash points between 100° and 150° F. (38°–65° C.).

HAZARDS

In addition to the general hazards of lighting and heating— naked flames, effect of heat on combustible materials, lighting-up, and the presence of flammable gases, vapours and dusts— described in Chapter XI, the following must be considered—

Filling. This should not be done when the burner is alight or still hot or when a flame is near. Care should be taken not to over-fill the reservoir or to spill oil. Portable lamps and stoves should be filled in a place set apart for the purpose, preferably in an outbuilding, over a metal tray to retain any spillage. It is very dangerous to use petrol in an appliance intended for paraffin.

Oil storage. Oil should be stored outside the main buildings to avoid the possibility of its assisting a fire which should break out in them. It should be kept in metal drums having draw-off taps.

Escape of oil due to defective equipment or, in some cases, because the appliance is not level or is exposed to a strong draught. Whenever possible oil heaters should stand in metal trays.

Portability. When any apparatus is portable, the likelihood of it and combustible material coming together is increased. With oil lamps or stoves there is the additional hazard that overturning may result in oil escaping from the reservoir and flaring up. Whenever possible they should be secured either to the floor or to heavy, wide baseplates so that they cannot easily be knocked over.

Lighting by Oil

There are now few places where gas or electricity are not available, but a surprisingly large number of people still use oil lamps, or even candles, for lighting. Candles should be fixed in candlesticks having large bases, and should be placed where it is impossible for combustible matter, e.g. curtains, to come into contact with them.

Oil lamps fall into two classes—

1. **Lamps burning oil at a wick.** These give either a luminous flame or, by the addition of air at the burner, a less luminous but hotter flame that heats a mantle to incandescence. The glass chimney serves to some extent to keep flammable materials away from the flame.

2. **Pressure lamps.** (Mineral oil vaporizing lamps.) A mantle is heated to incandescence by a non-luminous flame from a burner to which a mixture of air and oil vapour is supplied, the oil having been vaporized immediately before entering the burner. (Some pressure lamps are designed to use petrol.)

In one type a small hand pump is used to provide an air pressure in the oil reservoir. The oil is thus forced through a small nipple and turns to vapour in a tube set over the burner. Here it mixes with air, and reaches the burner as a vapour-air mixture. When the lamp is in action the vaporizing tube is kept hot, but on starting it must be warmed sufficiently to vaporize the oil; usually by igniting methylated spirit in a tray under the tube. Should the tube be insufficiently heated, oil instead of vapour is ejected and may flood the lamp.

Heating by Oil

The following types of oil-burning heating appliances, known as stoves, radiators, heaters, and so on are individually installed in the area to be heated.

1. **Stoves burning oil at a wick.** These burn kerosene (paraffin) and are usually portable. Some give a luminous white flame, others a non-luminous blue flame; the rate of burning is controlled by exposing more or less of the wick.

2. **Kindler type stoves (drip feed).** The rate of burning is varied by means of an adjustable valve which controls the flow of oil from the reservoir to a trough below the burner.   In the trough is an asbestos kindler at which the oil is ignited.

3. **Pressure stoves** do not need wicks or kindlers. A typical stove consists of an oil reservoir in which air-pressure is built up by the use of a small hand pump. The pressure forces the oil through a tube or neck where it is vaporized; the vapour passes through a nipple and mixes with air immediately under the burner, giving a non-luminous flame. When the stove is working the neck is kept sufficiently hot to vaporize the oil, but for starting it must be heated by burning methylated spirits in a cup fixed to the neck. Should the neck be insufficiently heated a jet of oil instead of vapour may be ejected from the nipple.

Most of these stoves are portable. They usually burn paraffin, but some are designed to burn petrol. It is dangerous to attempt to use petrol in a stove intended for paraffin.

Oil-fired space heaters are larger than the stoves previously mentioned, are fixed in one position, and have a flue. They comprise a burner, combustion chamber, heat exchanger, and a fan, and burn light oils with flash points of 38°–65° C. or 100°–150° F. In a typical air heater, a fan at the bottom draws in air, which on its passage upward is warmed by contact with the sides of a closed combustion chamber and in a tubular heat exchanger directly over the combustion chamber. The warm air leaves from outlets at the top part of the heater at a temperature of about 60° C. or 140° F. and is diffused away from it so as to be effective for some 50 ft. The gases from combustion are kept separate from the air and are taken away through a flue pipe. These heaters are usually installed inside buildings, but the hazard is reduced when they are placed in an outbuilding and the heated air passed to various parts of the building through ducting.

Oil Supply and Storage. The arrangements should be on the lines of those described under Storage Tanks, Oil Supply, and Fire Valves on pages 124–5. When a number of heaters is supplied from one tank long feed pipes may be unavoidable; sometimes they are in the form of a ring main inside the building from which a supply pipe is taken to each heater. The use of long pipes is undesirable, but it is even less satisfactory when the oil storage tank is inside the building.

Converted Stoves. Solid fuel stoves are sometimes converted to oil firing by installing an oil burner, supplied from a tank fixed near the stove. Some installations are well fitted up but in many cases arrangements are of such an improvised nature as to present considerable hazard. The tank should never be placed near enough to the stove to become heated or to enable oil which overflows or is spilt to reach the stove. It is undesirable that oil should be used to supplement solid fuel, as this practice is likely to lead to flaring or explosion.

Waste Oil. Garage proprietors and others sometimes use oil which has been drained from engines as a fuel for stoves. Hazards include the storage and handling of the oil. Its variable nature and water or foreign matter in it may lead to spasmodic action or blockage of burners not specially made for the purpose. The use of waste oil is discouraged by Fire Offices.

HEATING BY SOLID FUELS

Solid fuels, e.g. coal, coke, wood, are burnt either over hearths as open fires or in stoves which are partly or wholly enclosed. The hazards are those of naked flames, proximity of combustible materials, lighting up and the presence of flammable gases, vapours or dusts, which are described on pages 72–4.

FIREPLACES

An open fire produces the most comfortable and cheerful form of warmth and also ensures a measure of ventilation. The main types of open fires are those with metal bottoms to hold the fuel, set some inches above the hearth, and those known as "sunken" or "well" fires, where the fuel is burnt on, or in a well in, the fireclay base which actually rests on the hearth. When sunken fires are used the hearth gets much hotter than when there is an air space between the fire and the hearth.

Construction. The danger from the constructional features of a fireplace, i.e. the recess, hearth and chimney, is that of joists or other woodwork being insufficiently protected from the heat of the fire. In some old buildings the hearth rests on the wood joists which run under it to the wall. This practice is a cause of fires which could have been obviated by "trimming" the joists around the hearth, i.e. the joists which would otherwise pass under the hearth are cut short of the hearth and the cut ends supported on a "trimmer," which is itself supported on the "trimming joists" which reach the wall on the outsides of the chimney breast. The portion of the hearth known as the front hearth, which projects into the room, may be supported by a trimmer arch of brickwork, but by far the more usual method is to use a concrete slab.

Fenders or curbs serve two purposes—to prevent hot cinders from rolling from the hearth to wood flooring, and to prevent combustible materials, e.g. paper, cloth cuttings, etc., from finding their way on to the hearth. Metal fenders are generally suitable, but in cabinet makers' and similar workshops a fixed brick or concrete curb at least 12 in. in height is desirable.

Fireguards. Many deaths, particularly of children and elderly people, are caused by burns from clothing which has ignited by coming into contact with a fire. Articles being dried in front of an open fire by housewives, furriers and others are liable to be ignited by flying sparks.

A wire guard fixed to the fireplace surround prevents combustible materials from coming into contact with a fire, and if it has eight meshes to the inch also substantially reduces the danger from flying sparks. The guard should be of such a design that it need not be removed when the fire is refuelled or ashes are withdrawn.

Converted fireplaces and flues. Fire hazards often arise because a fireplace or flue which was suitable for its original purpose has been converted to another use. A flue adequate for a dwelling-room fire cannot safely be used for, say, a fish fryer's stove or a central heating boiler.

When a fireplace is disused it is not uncommon for it to be made up with wood or paper, but this is unsafe as sparks or burning soot from an adjoining flue may, in the event of the flue separations being defective, fall through the disused flue and ignite accumulated soot or the boarding up. The safe method of dealing with a disused fireplace is first to clear the flue of soot and then cover the opening with sheet metal, or, if desired, with brickwork.

STOVES

A large number of types of stoves burning coke, coal, or anthracite are included under this heading, the common feature being that they all have a pipe for carrying away smoke and providing a draught. All are provided with means of varying the draught by opening or closing dampers and some, known as *slow combustion stoves*, are so constructed that they will burn for many hours without attention. *Sawdust-burning stoves* are popular with woodworkers but not with fire offices, especially if, as is sometimes the case, the stoves are of flimsy construction.

Base. When a stove is over a wooden floor it must stand on a base or hearth of non-combustible material thick enough to protect the floor against heat. A sheet of metal is useless because heat is readily conducted through it. Fire offices are usually satisfied if the slab is of concrete or stone not less than 3 in. in thickness and extends well on each side and, particularly, in front, where ashes and cinders are likely to fall from the firing opening.

Fender or curb. A fixed metal fender or, preferably, a brick or concrete curb surrounding a stove prevents hot ashes and cinders from falling to the floor, and keeps paper, cuttings, waste, etc., away from the stove. In places such as printers', tailors', and woodworkers' shops a curb at least 6 in. in height should be constructed. Where articles are dried by the heat from the stove a substantial wire guard should be supplied in order to prevent any articles from coming into contact with the stove or its pipe.

Flue pipe. Whether the pipe discharges to a brick or concrete chimney or direct to the open, the shorter it is the better. Fire insurers sometimes charge an additional rate when a flue pipe exceeds a specified length, e.g. 3 ft.

Soot accumulates in the piping, especially at joints and in horizontal runs. Should the soot be ignited, the pipe may become hot enough to set fire to woodwork or other combustible material near it, or burning soot or sparks may escape from corroded or split portions of the piping or from badly fitting joints and fall on to combustible matter.

Cast-iron piping permits better joints to be made than does thin sheet metal, which, moreover, is subject to corrosion by coke fumes and is also attacked by the weather at the point where it passes through the roof, causing holes through which sparks may be emitted and rest among the roof timbers.

Asbestos-cement pipes are liable to crack from the heat passing through them or to be broken by impact. Only the heavy quality grade is satisfactory and even this should not be used for the first 6 ft. from the stove, where metal should be employed.

Woodwork near a stove. A stove should not be installed within 2 to 3 ft., according to the heat given out, of any woodwork, but if it is unavoidable to do so the wood must be protected by sheet iron or asbestos so fixed that there is an air space between the wood and the sheeting.

Flammable gases, vapours, and dusts. Where these are likely to be present no type of fire-heated stove is permissible.

PORTABLE COKE FIRES

These fires, which are variously known as cokels, devils, and braziers, are often constructed by punching holes in the sides and bottom of an ordinary bucket. They are a very hazardous form of heating, and should only be allowed in exceptional cases, e.g. foundry casting shops. They emit sparks, are quite unprotected against contact of combustible materials, and are liable to be knocked over.

BUILDING REGULATIONS

The installation of any of the heating appliances described in this chapter is controlled by the Building Regulations 1965. Class I includes any solid fuel or oil-burning appliance having an output rating not exceeding 150,000 British Thermal Units per hour; an appliance of greater output is called a High Rating Appliance. The provisions apply also to solid fuel fires which burn on a hearth without any appliance. As the regulations are not retrospective, appliances installed before 1966 may not comply with all of them and in these cases fire insurers must decide whether to be satisfied with the existing arrangements.

A general requirement is that any chimney, flue pipe, constructional hearth or fireplace recess shall be (*a*) constructed of non-combustible materials of such a nature, quality, and thickness as not to be unduly affected by heat, condensate or the products of combustion; and (*b*) so constructed and of such thickness, or in the case of a flue pipe, so placed or shielded, as to prevent the ignition of any part of the building.

Fireplace recess. The jambs and back to be not less than 8 in. thick but if the recess is in an external wall or where two fireplaces on opposite sides of a wall (other than a wall separating buildings or dwellings within a building) have a common back, the back may be not less than 4 in. thick.

Hearths to be not less than 5 in. thick. If the hearth adjoins a floor of combustible material it must (*a*) if in a fireplace recess, project not less than 20 in. in front of the jambs and extend at each side not less than 6 in. beyond the opening or (*b*) if not in a fireplace recess, be large enough to contain a square whose sides measure not less than 2 ft. 6 in. The distance from the front of the heating appliance to the edge of the hearth must be not less than 9 in. or, if it is an open fire or a stove which can be opened to operate as an open fire, not less than 12 in. The back and sides of the appliance must not be within 6 in. of the edge of the hearth. The upper surface of a hearth in contact with a combustible floor must not be lower than the floor and there must not be any combustible material under a hearth within 10 in., measured vertically, of the surface of the hearth.

Walls and partitions within 6 in. of a hearth must be not less than 3 in. thick of non-combustible material to a height of 4 ft. above the hearth. If such wall is within 6 in. of any part of the appliance it must extend to a height of 12 in. above the appliance and if within 2 in. its thickness must be 12 in. Moreover, any part of the building constructed of combustible material must be protected so that it will not be ignited by heat from the appliance.

Chimneys and flues. A flue is a passage for conveying the discharge, i.e. smoke, gases, etc., of an appliance to the external air. The term includes pipes and also chimneys, which are any part of the structure forming part of a flue other than a flue pipe. A flue must be provided for any appliance other than an oil-burning one not exceeding 10,000 B.T.U. per hour, e.g. portable oil stove.

Flue pipes must be so constructed, placed or shielded as to prevent the ignition of any part of a building and that there is no undue risk of accidental damage to the pipe or danger to persons. They must be properly supported and discharge either into a chimney or into the external air. They must not pass through any roof space, floor, internal wall or partition except through a floor supporting a chimney or a wall forming part of a chimney so as, in each case, to discharge into that chimney.

A flue pipe passing through an external wall or roof must be at a distance of not less than three times its external diameter from any combustible material or be suitably protected, e.g. (*a*) by solid non-combustible material not less than 8 in. thick (or if the combustible material is above the pipe, 12 in. (*b*) enclosed in a sleeve of metal or asbestos-cement sheeting projecting 6 in. beyond any combustible material in the wall or roof, the space between the sleeve and the pipe being not less than 1 in., packed with non-combustible thermal insulating material, e.g. asbestos.

If a flue pipe is within a distance of less than three times its external diameter of combustible material in an internal wall or partition it must be protected, e.g. by a shield of non-combustible material so placed that there is an air space of not less than ½ in. between the shield and the combustible material, or fixed between the wall and the pipe so that it projects on each side of the pipe.

Chimneys must be not less than 4 in. thick and have specified linings, e.g. clay flue linings. A chimney may contain more than one flue, each of which must be surrounded by solid material 4 in. thick. Where a chimney is in a wall separating buildings (or dwellings within a building) and is not back to back with another chimney, the back must be not less than 8 in. thick. No combustible material may be built into walls within 6 in. of a flue in a chimney.

CHAPTER XIII

LIGHTING AND HEATING BY GAS

A NUMBER of gases are capable of use for lighting and heating purposes, but in practice town gas is so predominant that it is referred to without ambiguity simply as "gas." It is produced from coal, petroleum and other sources by public authorities in gas works and distributed to consumers by way of gas mains.

The hazards of gas can be considered under two heads: the risk in distributing the gas throughout the building and the risks at the appliances using it. The predominant feature in both cases is that in the event of leakage and mixture with air a flammable and explosive mixture may be formed which can easily be ignited by any naked flame, fire, electric spark, or even by some ignorant person looking for the leakage with a lighted candle or match. Fortunately gas has a pungent smell, which discloses its presence.

GAS INSTALLATIONS

The first requirement to avoid trouble is that the installation be carried out by reputable contractors and that first-class materials are used. All piping should be iron, steel, or copper, and separated by spacing or insulation from any electrical conduit, cable or appliance. Fires have occurred where, due to electrolysis or electric arcs, gas piping has been punctured and the leaking gas ignited.

Whenever possible rigid piping should be used but, in the case of portable appliances, e.g. irons, pokers, rings, this is not practicable. In these cases good quality metallic tubing should be used, screwed at one end to the appliance and at the other end to a plug. The plug is fixed when required into a socket on the permanent piping, in which a shut-off tap should be installed. All gas taps should be of a type that cannot be turned on accidentally.

Meters should be placed in accessible, ventilated positions and clear of combustible materials. A fire near the meter is likely to melt the supply piping, which at this point is of heavy lead to permit of easy installation and removal of meters. A cupboard under the staircase cannot be regarded as a suitable situation.

Sometimes the manager of a premises will assert with the pride of rectitude that "gas and electricity are shut off at the meters every night." While there is a good deal to be said for this practice, there is an objection to it, inasmuch as a subsidiary tap—

say to a soldering stove—may have been left on at night. When the main stop cock is opened next morning gas may escape from the stove unobserved. Similarly, electric apparatus may unwittingly become "alive." There is, however, no doubt as to the desirability of having the main gas stop cock and electric switches plainly indicated in such a place that they are accessible to the fire service without delay, yet not easily reached by unauthorized persons. It is necessary that such cocks be maintained in good order—cases have been known where, from lack of use, they have become so corroded that when required in a hurry they cannot be turned. Any taps likely to be accidentally knocked on should be of the "drop handle" type or have removable keys.

Reference was made in Chapter XI to the hazards of lighting up (which can in the case of gas be obviated by the use of by-pass lights), naked flames, portable appliances, proximity of combustible materials, and the presence of flammable gases, vapours, and dust, any or all of which are applicable to gas lighting and heating.

GAS APPLIANCES

The heating appliances mentioned in this chapter are those which are individually installed in the area or space to be heated. Their installation is controlled by the Building Regulations 1965, see pages 89–90.

Gas burners for lighting. Occasionally a burner using a luminous flame is found, but almost all burners are of the type using a non-luminous flame to heat a mantle, which gives a much better light and more heat than a luminous flame. It is possible for glowing fragments to fall, perhaps on to flammable material.

Gas fires use a row of bunsen type burners to heat asbestos "elements" to redness. Wire guards should be fitted. If the fire is not on a proper hearth, a stone slab should be provided to protect wood flooring under and in front of it.

Gas radiant heaters are similar to gas fires but are usually fixed overhead.

Gas unit heaters consist of a metal casing containing a fan by which air is forced through gas "elements" and distributed in the direction desired.

Provided radiant and unit heaters are permanently fixed in positions where no combustible material, e.g. roof lining, is endangered they form a good method of heating by gas as the burners are not in the way of floor waste, etc.

Gas radiators consist of a number of vertical metal columns set above a row of bunsen type burners which heat the air in the columns and thus the columns themselves. The term *radiator* is a misnomer as the atmosphere of the room is warmed by contact with the hot metal columns, i.e. by convection rather than by radiation. In some gas radiators a small quantity of water is contained in the bottom of the columns, which are then heated not by air but by steam vaporized by heat from the burners. Gas radiators should stand on a stone or concrete slab to protect the wood flooring but, in general, are safer than open gas fires as the burners are more or less enclosed in the base and so there is less likelihood of combustible material coming into contact with them.

Garage type gas radiators. The enclosure of the ordinary radiator is not sufficient to exclude flammable vapours, but for use in garages and other places where such vapours are likely two special types are obtainable. In both types the burners are entirely enclosed in the base of the radiator, the difference lying in the manner in which the air necessary for the operation of the burners is introduced. In one type it enters the combustion chamber through orifices which are protected with wire gauze on the principle of the *Davy miner's safety lamp*. Any flammable mixtures of vapour and air which enter through the orifices may ignite and burn inside the radiator, but the flame will not travel through the gauze because the wire cools the mixture below its ignition temperature. One disadvantage of this type is that the gauze may become clogged or broken, in which state it ceases to be a protection. The other type is a "room-sealed appliance" which draws air from and discharges products of combustion to the atmosphere outside the building. The inlet, outlet and combustion chamber are enclosed and thus isolated from the room in which the appliance is situated. In both types access to the burners for lighting them in the first place is obtained by the removal of a screwed cap. A by-pass jet is allowed to burn continually so that the burners may be re-lit without removing this screwed cap. It will be appreciated that when the cap is not in position the exposed opening renders useless the safety precautions and the radiator is at the same disadvantage with regard to flammable vapours as any ordinary radiator.

Gas rings are used for many purposes such as boiling kettles and heating glue pots, irons, etc. It is common to find them on wood benches or shelves which are either bare or covered only with thin metal or asbestos cement sheeting. This is unsatisfactory: the removal of the covering often discloses that the woodwork beneath is charred. A base of stone or concrete 2 in. thick should be provided and the whole placed in a metal tray with sides sufficiently high to prevent combustible matter from being swept against the ring. Alternatively, the ring can safely be placed on a metal

4

stand at least 12 in. in height. Flexible tubing is generally used to connect gas rings, but rigid piping is much safer, both inherently and because it ensures that the ring will remain on its base.

Gas heated enamelling and other ovens. See pages 110–12.

Other gas heated appliances include wash boilers, washing machines and water heaters. Instantaneous water heaters are usually fixed to a wall above a sink and when turned on provide a stream of hot water. Storage water heaters heat a quantity of water and store it in an insulated tank.

Storage of Gas

It is unusual for gas to be stored elsewhere than at gas works. Until recent years all gas holders were of the watersealed type, the appearance of which is familiar to everyone. An inverted circular steel shell rises and falls, according to the quantity of gas contained, in a water-filled pit or tank below ground level. The water acts as a seal to prevent the gas from escaping. These gas holders may have a single "lift" (or section) or several lifts arranged telescopically.

Most of the gas holders in this country are of this type, but there are also a number of "waterless" gasholders. These are much larger than the waterseal type and consist externally of a fixed polygonal shell of steel plates. The gas is contained between the concrete base and a "piston" or false roof which fits closely to the sides of the shell and rises or falls according to whether gas is being admitted or withdrawn. It is important that the gas shall not leak from the lower portion into the air space above the piston, as were this to occur an explosive mixture would be formed capable of ignition by a spark or flame. This is a hazard not present in the waterseal type and to prevent such leakage a trough of tar is attached to the periphery of the piston, providing a film of tar (or tar seal) between it and the sides of the shell.

The safety of either type is dependent on the gas being precluded from mixing with air, and the main danger to be apprehended is that of a fire or explosion, occurring nearby, so severely damaging the gasholder that such mixture could take place. The large size of the waterless gasholders, ranging from one to ten million cubic feet, is a disadvantage from this point of view.

Liquefied Petroleum Gases

Where town gas is unobtainable it is possible, nevertheless, to enjoy the conveniences of gas lighting and heating by using liquefied petroleum gases. These gases, largely *butane* or *propane*, are liquids when under pressure, but vaporize when the pressure is released.

Calor gas is the proprietary name of a butane mixture supplied in cylinders about 23 in. high by 13 in. diameter in which the gas is in liquid form, being under a moderate pressure of about 23 lb. per sq. in. (one-and-a-half atmospheres). When the pressure is released the liquid changes to gas, in which form it is distributed to the appliances. Practically any equipment used for coal gas can be adjusted for calor gas, and the hazards of the various appliances are similar.

As the gas is very penetrating, great care must be taken with joints and taps, neither red lead, solder, nor ordinary rubber being allowable. Mixtures of 1·9 per cent to 8·6 per cent of the gas with air are flammable, so that a very small leak may be dangerous. Leakage is most likely to occur at the cylinder valve or the connection between the cylinder and the burner, or when cylinders are being changed. Pure butane, has no smell and an odorant is added to facilitate detection of leakages. Where a number of appliances (e.g. lighting burners, cooker, etc.) are installed, copper or iron piping is used to convey the gas from the cylinder to the appliances, but when only one or two appliances are to be supplied flexible tubing is used.

Other liquefied petroleum gases may be regarded similarly. Their use in industry for process heating and other purposes is increasing.

Storage. Gas containers should be stored with the valve uppermost, not in the main buildings but in a detached, unheated, well-ventilated store. They should not be stored below ground level or where gas, which is heavier than air, could drift through drains, culverts or openings leading to cellars or other places where gas might accumulate. In fighting a fire involving gas it is not enough to extinguish the flames; if the gas is not turned off at its source its continuing escape presents a serious hazard.

ACETYLENE

When calcium carbide—a grey substance manufactured by combining coke dust and lime in an electric furnace—and water are brought together heat is developed and a gas known as acetylene is generated, leaving behind spent lime in the form of sludge. Acetylene was at one time used for lighting buildings in out of the way places, such as country mansions, when burners similar to coal gas burners were used but it is doubtful whether any such installations still exist. The gas is, however, freely used for metal welding and cutting purposes because a mixture of oxygen and acetylene burned in a suitable blowpipe produces a flame hot enough to melt all common metals (see pages 137–8). Acetylene gas forms a flammable and explosive mixture with air in proportions

ranging from as low as 3 per cent acetylene—97 per cent air to as
high as 82 per cent acetylene—18 per cent air. This range is
greater than that of any other gas, and even a slight leak is likely
to have grave consequences; fortunately the gas has a distinctive
odour, rather like garlic. No metal containing more than 80 per
cent of copper should be used in any pipe, valve, or other fitting as
the action of acetylene on copper is to form copper acetylide,
which is a highly explosive compound readily detonated by heat
or friction.

Acetylene is not supplied through mains by supply undertakings, but cylinders of this gas can be purchased, or when
large volumes are required a generating plant is installed.

Acetylene generators are of various types, the main difference
being in the method by which the water and carbide are brought
together. Considerable heat is evolved in the generation of the
gas, and faulty design of apparatus may permit high temperatures
and unsafe pressures to develop, after which an explosion may
occur.

Situation. Generating plants should be either in the open or
in a well-ventilated shed used for no other purpose and having
no communication with any other building. Only authorized
persons should have access to the shed.

Any artificial lighting should be outside the building, the light
entering through fixed plate-glass windows. Heating should be
limited to low-pressure steam or hot-water pipes, the boiler being
outside the building. No naked lights may be taken into a
generator house or near a generator in the open, and smoking
should be strictly prohibited.

Sludge (spent carbide). It often happens that the centres of
large lumps of carbide are not exhausted when withdrawn from
the generator. If the sludge is placed in a damp situation acetylene will continue to be evolved and an explosive atmosphere
may arise. Care, therefore, should be taken that the sludge is
deposited in a safe, remote place in proper settling tanks.

Storage of calcium carbide. Bearing in mind that moisture,
even the moisture of the air, will cause calcium carbide to give
off acetylene, care in storage is necessary. The storeroom should
be a detached, perfectly dry, well-ventilated shed in which the
metal airtight drums in which carbide is stored are raised above
the ground. Steel tools must not be used to open the drums as
a spark may be caused and any acetylene gas in the drum ignited.
Special tools with bronze points should be used. No smoking or
naked flames may be permitted in the vicinity and arrangements
for lighting and heating should be similar to those for generator
houses. A prominent warning of the nature of the store should be

displayed in order that water shall not be used in attempts to extinguish a fire or for any other reason.

Dissolved acetylene. Most users of acetylene avoid the trouble and hazards of generating it by purchasing the gas in cylinders.

At pressures over $3\frac{1}{2}$ lb. per sq. in. acetylene is spontaneously explosive and its use or storage in this state is prohibited by law. It is, therefore, impossible to compress it in cylinders in the way that oxygen or hydrogen is treated. Its conveyance would be difficult indeed were it not for the fact that when dissolved in acetone it can be subjected to considerable pressure without having explosive properties; under this treatment it is known as dissolved acetylene. Although the acetylene is not spontaneously explosive in this state, the cylinders must not be subjected to rough usage, shocks, or high temperatures.

Precautions which should be taken when acetylene is used for metal cutting and welding (for which purposes it is more used than for lighting) are dealt with on pages 137–8.

BUILDING REGULATIONS

The installation of any of the heating appliances described in this chapter is controlled by the Building Regulations 1965. Class II includes any gas appliance having an input rating not exceeding 150,000 British Thermal Units per hour and an appliance of greater rating is called a High Rating appliance.

A general requirement is that any chimney, flue pipe, constructional hearth or fireplace recess shall be (a) constructed of non-combustible materials of such a nature, quality and thickness as not to be unduly affected by heat, condensate or the products of combustion and (b) so constructed and of such thickness, or in the case of a flue pipe, so placed or shielded, as to prevent the ignition of any part of the building.

Hearths. Appliances must stand on a hearth of non-combustible material not less than $\frac{1}{2}$ in. thick extending 6 in. beyond the back and sides and forward 9 in. from any flame or incandescent material within the appliance, unless it is installed so that no flame or incandescent material is less than 9 in. above the floor. The back, sides and top of the appliance must be separated from any combustible material forming part of the building by a shield of non-combustible material not less than 1 in. thick or an air space of 3 in.

Chimneys are to be suitably lined, e.g. with acid resisting tiles or vitrified clay pipes. Any flue in a chimney is to be surrounded by solid material not less than 1 in. thick and there must not be any fastening, other than a non-combustible support to a flue liner, within 1 in. of the flue. The length of a flue is limited according to the type of appliance and the situation of the flue.

Flue pipes. Materials allowed include cast iron, sheet steel and asbestos-cement, all to conform to the appropriate British Standard and be coated on the inside with acid resistant enamel or compound. The pipe must be safely placed or shielded. This requirement is satisfied if, for example, no part of the pipe is within 2 in. of any combustible material and where it passes through a roof, floor, ceiling wall or partition constructed of combustible material it is enclosed in a sleeve of non-combustible material and separated from the sleeve by an air space of 1 in. or more.

The size of flues is controlled in detail. For example, the cross-sectional area of a gas fire flue is to be not less than 20 square inches and of any other appliance not less than the area of its outlet. A table gives details for flues serving more than one appliance. No openings may be made into flues other than those for inspection and cleaning fitted with a gas tight cover.

A gas cooker may discharge into the room in which it is situated. In general, any other appliance must discharge into a flue but, under specified conditions which vary according to the type and input rating of the appliance, a room-sealed appliance (one whose inlet, outlet and combustion chamber are isolated from the room), a gas heater in an airing or drying cupboard, a water heater or a space heating appliance, e.g. a fire need not vent into a flue provided the room has an openable window and a permanent vent to the open air.

CHAPTER XIV

LIGHTING AND HEATING BY ELECTRICITY

IT is not possible to compress into a reasonable space an explanation of the theory and principles of electricity, a subject which demands a library of its own. This chapter must be confined to a mention of the more common appliances and an explanation of how fires are caused by their use. It is assumed that most readers have a knowledge of the elementary principles of electricity; any who have no knowledge of the subject may find it simplest to compare the flow of electricity with the flow of water, although the analogy is far from complete.

Electricity is a force which man utilizes to do work for him, such as heating a wire to red heat to provide warmth or heating a filament to incandescence to give light. Pressure (measured in *volts*) and rate of flow (measured in *amperes*) may be thought of in a similar manner to the pressure and rate of flow of water.

CONDUCTORS AND CIRCUITS

Substances through which electricity flows easily are known as *conductors*, and those which oppose its passage are called *insulators*. A cable or a flexible cord consists of a conductor (e.g. copper wire or wires) through which an electric current can pass, enclosed in an insulating covering (e.g. rubber) which prevents the electricity from leaking. Excessive pressure, overheating, age, damp or mechanical damage will cause the insulation to break down and permit leakage.

Electricity will flow only in a closed circuit, i.e. there must be a conductor from the generator to the appliance in use and another by means of which it can return to the generator. These will be referred to as live and neutral respectively. As electricity flows only in a closed circuit the current can be started or stopped by closing opening the circuit at any point, e.g. by using a switch, which for safety must be in the live conductor.

As no conductor is perfect, the current has to overcome some resistance (even as water has to overcome friction in pipes) and the energy thus spent is shown as heat. The longer the conductor or the thinner it is or the poorer the conducting quality of the material used, the greater is the resistance, and therefore the greater the heat which arises. The relationship in the circuit between pressure and resistance, i.e. the combined resistance of the wiring and of all appliances which can be included in the circuit, must be such that the current does not exceed that which it is safe for the wiring to carry. Actually the current is proportional to the pressure (electromotive force) divided by the resistance. The amount of heat produced is directly in proportion to the resistance multiplied by the square of the current. Thus, if a circuit carries three times the current for which it was designed the heating effect is nine times as great. Such heat may be sufficient to lead to breakdown and subsequent ignition of the insulation.

One of the most important features from a fire prevention point of view is that there shall be no escape of this heat producer —electricity—and for this reason all conductors must be efficiently insulated. Moisture causes insulation to deteriorate and can cause short circuits and earth faults.

Short circuits. Should the insulation break down or any other circumstance (such as a nail driven into a wall and touching both conductors) allow current to flow directly from the live to the neutral conductor without passing through the appliances in the circuit the current will take this path of less resistance in preference to its appointed route, and as there is less resistance, greater current will flow with the accompaniment of much greater heat than was intended, perhaps enough to ignite combustible materials nearby. When the current leaks from the live conductor and finds its way back to its source, not through the negative conductor at all but by way of earth, the type of short circuit is known as an earth fault.

Fuses. To limit the current which can flow through a circuit fuses are provided. These may be short lengths of soft wire placed in non-combustible holders and so constituted that they will fuse or melt should excessive current flow, thus breaking the circuit and stopping the flow of electricity before the wiring can become dangerously hot.

When a fuse "blows" it suggests that there is a fault in the wiring or the appliances connected to it; if when the fuse is replaced by a new one it blows again the suggestion becomes a certainty. The proper procedure then is to rectify the fault. If the fuse were replaced by a larger one, or, as is unfortunately sometimes done, by ordinary thick wire, the protection which should be afforded by the fuse acting as a safety valve is lost.

It is essential for safety that all circuits are properly protected by fuses. The current required to cause a fuse to operate varies with the circumstances and the regulations of the Institution of Electrical Engineers indicate the size of fuse required.

Many so-called electricians imagine that provided proper fuses are supplied, it is impossible for the wiring to overheat, but this is not correct. If wiring becomes corroded its effective size is reduced and in this state it is not able safely to carry as large a current as it could carry in its original condition. The fuse, however, would still permit as large a current to flow as it did originally, and this current, although safe enough with the wire when new, may be sufficient to overheat the wire when its size has been reduced by corrosion. If the corroded wire then breaks, a spark or arc is formed. Owing to the resistance of the air in the gap between the broken ends, the current may not be large enough to blow the fuse, but yet be enough to maintain the arc, which may be regarded as a continuous spark.

Arcs may similarly occur whenever live and neutral conductors, the insulation of which has become useless through age or misuse, momentarily come into contact with each other and then separate; or, when a live conductor touches and then parts slightly from earthed metal, e.g. a gas pipe. Arcs can also occur at badly-made joints, switches and elsewhere. They have a high temperature and combustible materials near them are easily ignited.

Earthing. All metal forming part of an installation (except, of course, the conductors), e.g. conduit, frames of appliances, etc., must be connected to earth to provide a safe and easy path for any leakage of current. The lower the resistance of the path, the sooner will an earth fault cause the fuses to operate.

Workmanship and materials. It can safely be asserted that most electrical fires are caused by defects in wiring and fittings. Perhaps the materials used were not of good quality or "economy" was exercised in utilizing conductors barely sufficient to carry the required current, without consideration of the fact that consumers almost invariably wish to add further appliances subsequently. Foresight in providing for reasonable numbers of socket outlets would often obviate overloading in the future. Bad workmanship may have left joints in an unsafe condition or good cable may have been damaged during installation.

Too often, although the original installation is satisfactory, alterations and extensions are made by incompetent persons. Even if the wiring is reasonably done the extension may result in overloading and consequent overheating of the original wiring, but frequently extensions are made with flexible cords. There are various grades of flex ranging from poor stuff, unsuitable for any purpose, through types appropriate for use where no mechanical damage is likely, e.g. for connecting lampholders to ceiling roses, to types of high insulation cords with protective coverings suitable for use with portable appliances. The higher grades are permissible for temporary extensions, but the danger arises that an extension originally intended to be temporary often becomes a permanent one. It is good practice to regard any form of flex as unsuitable for fixed wiring. It must not in any case be run out of sight (e.g. behind fixtures or under carpets), and should be supported on porcelain hooks or cleats; certainly not by nails or ordinary staples.

INSPECTIONS

Electric supply undertakings carry out a test of an installation before they supply current, but when that has been done they appear to take no interest in the installation apart from reading the meter and collecting the money. It has been suggested that they should be obliged to make periodical tests, and while it may be open to question whether it would be reasonable to impose this duty on the undertakings, there is no doubt that many fires would be prevented by regular inspections and tests.

All installations should conform in every detail to the " Regulations for the electrical equipment of buildings" of the Institution of Electrical Engineers, which are supported by insurance companies and supply undertakings. The Insurance Surveyor or Fire Service Officer who is called upon for a general report on a premises may not have available, at the time, apparatus for making a test, but there are some features which may be observed during a cursory inspection to enable a decision to be made whether a detailed examination and test are desirable, e.g. any obvious deterioration of insulation.

It is not possible to state the period during which an installation may be regarded as safe, as this depends not only on the quality of the materials used and the degree of workmanship in their installation, but also upon whether the wiring has been subjected to heat or damp and upon the other conditions prevailing. An inspection and a test by a Chartered Electrical Engineer or other competent person should be carried out at intervals of not more than three to five years. He should report on the insulation, earthing, condition of cables, flexible cords, switches, fuses, plugs and socket-outlets, any signs of overloading of conductors or accessories, and point out any obvious defects.

WIRING SYSTEMS

Bare wiring. It is unusual for bare conductors, i.e. those without an insulating covering, to be used, but where they are installed they must not ordinarily be accessible to unauthorized persons, must be carried on effective insulators, adequately spaced, and out of contact with any part of the building.

Cleated wiring (exposed). Braided vulcanized india-rubber or p.v.c. insulated cables can be used without casing or conduit providing they are open to view throughout, and are supported on effective insulators so spaced as to prevent the cables coming into contact with each other or with any part of the building. Where passing through floors, walls, etc., they must be enclosed in metal or other suitable conduit.

Metal-sheathed cables must be supported by types of clips, saddles or clamps which will not damage the cables and so spaced as to prevent sagging. The sheathing must be electrically continuous and earthed.

Tough rubber-protected cables and polyvinylchloride (p.v.c.) covered cables must be supported similarly. Rubber burns freely; p.v.c. with difficulty but melts at a fairly low temperature.

Metal conduit. It is probable that for general use the safest form of wiring is that in which the cables are enclosed in screwed metal conduit. The conduit must be earthed and must be electrically and mechanically continuous, either by means of screwed joints or of grips to retain rigidity. Inspection and connection boxes are of metal and connected by screwing the conduit into the side of the box. Slip socket conduit is unsatisfactory as the lengths of conduit may become separated and lose earthing continuity, while the rough edges may damage the insulation of the cables. All conduits must be erected to avoid as far as possible condensation of moisture, which would rust the conduit and cause the cable insulation to deteriorate.

Mineral insulated copper sheathed cable. The insulation is of compressed magnesia or other mineral insulation and the whole of the cable is thus of non-combustible materials. The ends must be sealed against moisture.

Wood casing should be secured by screws and used only in dry situations. It is, of course, combustible, and it is possible for nails to be driven into it accidentally and damage the cables inside. This method is obsolete.

Flexible cords should be discouraged as fixed wiring, but if installed, for sub-circuits only, they should be of the high insulation type, in view for the whole of their length and supported on effective insulators at intervals of not more than 3 ft.

Mechanical damage. In every form of wiring the cables, conduit, etc., must be adequately protected against mechanical damage, especially within 6 ft. of the floor. Where passing through floors or walls the holes should be made good with non-combustible materials so that space is not left through which fire might spread. Cables and conduit must be prevented by spacing, insulation, or other means from coming into contact with gas and water pipes. Fires have occurred when direct current has been used because a gas pipe in a damp situation has become so affected by electrolytic action as to be punctured and the escaping gas has been ignited by an electric spark. A gas pipe must on no account be used as an "earth." In damp situations supports and fixings of insulators should be of non-rusting material.

Joints, if badly made, are a cause of overheating of wiring and of arcs. When, as sometimes happens, two cables are merely twisted together, covered with insulation tape and tucked away out of sight, the only question is how long it will be before trouble arises. Joints involving a flexible cord may only be made by means of mechanical connectors, but all other connections between cables may be made either by means of a mechanical connector or by a soldered joint. All joints should be enclosed in joint boxes or fittings suitable to the form of wiring. The fewer the joints the better from the fire prevention point of view.

Switchboards should be of a durable, non-ignitable and non-absorbent nature and placed in a dry, well-ventilated situation where rubbish and other combustible materials cannot accumulate.

Fuses must be so arranged that no molten metal can come into contact with combustible materials. The size of the fuse is determined by the *smallest* cable in the circuit in order that all cables are protected against overheating. Replacing a blown fuse with a larger one means that the wiring may be unprotected.

Switches must have a quick break action or an arc may be set up between the contacts. A single pole switch must be fitted to the live conductor: a double pole switch operates on both. Switches should not be fitted within 4 ft. 6 in. of the floor in garages on account of the possibility of the presence of petrol vapour, which is heavier than air.

Plugs and socket-outlets. The appearance of plugs and sockets for connecting portable appliances to the supply are well known, but the hazards associated with them are not so well appreciated. Many portable appliances are provided with a built-in switch by means of which the apparatus can be switched off. If this is done the flexible wiring connecting the appliance to the plug remains alive, and as such flexibles are subject to much wear it is not surprising that fires occur by reason of flexible cords becoming damaged. They often run over, or even under, carpets and rugs, and should a short circuit occur in them, or some of the strands of wire of which they are composed break, leaving the few remaining intact to carry the whole of the current, the insulation may ignite and in turn fire combustible materials in contact with it. All socket outlets should be provided with switches in order that the flexible cord need not be alive when the appliance is not in use. Such switches are, of course, of no avail unless they are operated and unless they are inserted in the live conductor.

To reduce the possibilities of shock, three-pin plugs, which enable portable appliances to be earthed, are preferable to the two-pin type, and, moreover, the plugs cannot be inserted "the wrong way round." A socket outlet should not be fitted in or near a floor, where it could be affected by water used in washing the floor.

Socket-outlet adaptors can be used to supply several appliances (e.g. a radio set, a table lamp, and a fire) from one socket but the practice is objectionable as the circuit may be overloaded or one of the appliances may become switched on inadvertently. One of the many fires which have been caused in this fashion happened in an office where an electric fire and a duplicating machine were operated from one switch-controlled socket with a two-way adaptor. The fire had been in use, and after it had been duly switched off at the socket it was placed in a corner against some papers stacked on the floor. Subsequently a typist plugged into the unoccupied side of the adaptor the plug of the duplicator and switched on the current, which of course caused not only the duplicator but the fire as well to become alive. The papers stacked against it ignited and as a result of the fire the girl lost her life. A separate socket should be supplied for each appliance in use. It is not a good practice to connect appliances to lamp-holders, as not only is the wiring liable to be overloaded but the connection made is a poor one.

Lighting Appliances

Incandescent lamps. As the filament is enclosed in a sealed glass globe and there is no "naked" light, electric lamps are safer than any other source of light, but it must not be overlooked that the glass may become hot enough to ignite dust, fluff, or other flammable materials in contact with it. Celluloid is particularly dangerous, but paper or textile lamp shades and curtains, etc., should not be allowed to touch the lamps. When electric lamps are enclosed in recesses to provide concealed lighting effects there is a possibility of woodwork becoming dangerously heated.

Luminous discharge lamps (fluorescent tubes) contain a gas which becomes luminous when a current is passed through it. To start them, they require a higher voltage than that at which they normally operate; for this an automatic switch and an induction coil, or choke, are provided. As either of these might become overheated and ignite nearby materials they should preferably be enclosed either in the lighting fitting assembly or in a suitably designed non-combustible enclosure or else so mounted that no unprotected wood or other combustible material is within 12 in. above or within 6 in. in any other direction. The exterior of the tubes is cooler than that of an ordinary incandescent lamp but as sparks are possible at lamp-holders and other connections the lamps are unsuitable for use where flammable vapours, gases or dusts are likely unless they have flameproof fittings.

HEATING APPLIANCES

Fires or radiators of the type in which a coiled wire element is heated to redness are the most common. The heat is sufficient to ignite combustible materials which come into contact with the elements or are in close proximity to them. Insurance companies are quite accustomed to claims for trousers or skirts that have been ruined because their wearers were standing too close to an electric fire, and for articles being dried in front of one. Regulations under the Heating Appliances (Fireguards) Act, 1952, require that appropriate guards shall be fitted to electric heaters of types suitable for use in dwellings if, without a guard, there would be a likelihood of injury by burning. In the type of heater known as a convector the heating elements are within a metal casing that serves as a guard.

Portable fires have the disadvantages that flexible wiring must be used, that the fire may be overturned, and that it may be placed near combustible materials.

Non-luminous (black heat) radiators are those whose outer casing does not attain red heat; usually the temperature is around 200° F. or 93° C. Some consist of heating elements completely enclosed in a metal case and others, known as *oil-filled radiators* comprise a sealed container filled with oil which is heated by an electric immersion heater. These types have the advantage that the external surfaces do not ordinarily attain dangerously high temperatures but, like tubular heaters and thermal storage heaters, they may do so if they become covered up, e.g. with curtains, clothing, etc.

Tubular heaters comprise metal tubes or casings some feet in length, enclosing a heating element on porcelain or fire clay supports, which prevent the element from touching the metal case. The tubes are mounted on brackets, usually on skirting boards, and should be so fixed as to be clear of woodwork.

Unit heaters. A metal casing contains coiled wire elements, which usually operate at black heat, and a fan that provides a current of air through the elements and distributes the heated air. They are fitted overhead, and are thus out of the way of floor waste and so on. Care must be taken that there is no wood-work or other combustible material near the heaters.

Thermal storage heaters, or night storage heaters, consist of heating elements embedded in a firebrick composition surrounded by blocks of concrete or firebrick, the whole contained in a sheet metal case. A time switch allows the blocks to be heated only at night, when cheap current is available, and the accumulated heat is given off throughout the following day. Unless there is a free circulation of air around the heater its temperature may rise sufficiently to ignite combustible materials in contact with it; a strong wire mesh guard should therefore be so fixed as to ensure that a clear space of 3 in. from all surfaces of the heater is main-tained. Some of these heaters are thermostatically controlled.

Heating cable systems, which are designed to attain a low temperature, are either run in panels for fixing to walls and ceilings or embedded in floors. When installed in concrete floors, a tubular metal housing is laid on the floor and then embedded in a layer of concrete screed on which the floor finish is applied later. The heating cables, which generally consist of lead-sheathed twin conductors having moisture- and heat-resisting insulation, are drawn through the embedded housing.

The system is thermostatically controlled and the cables do not normally attain a high temperature, but they should nevertheless be fixed well clear of combustible material.

Electric irons. Apart from the hazards previously mentioned in connection with flexible wiring and plugs and sockets, there is the added possibility of the iron, while still switched on, being placed and allowed to remain on combustible material. Many of the fires which have occurred in this manner would have been avoided had a suitable stand of thick non-combustible material been provided and a pilot light been in use.

Pilot (or warning) lights are lamps, generally coloured red, installed in the same circuit as an appliance so that the lamp is always alight when the controlling switch is on. (A lamp that operates with the thermostat in a heat-controlled iron or other appliance does not achieve the same purpose because it is alight only intermittently.) Irons and cooking ovens should always be provided with pilot lights, and the precaution might well be extended to other apparatus which gives no obvious sign when it is alive.

FLAMMABLE ATMOSPHERES AND FLAMEPROOF APPARATUS

It is impracticable entirely to exclude a flammable atmosphere from a fitting. The term "flameproof" means that if gas enters and is ignited inside the enclosure the flame will not be communicated to the external atmosphere. This is achieved by making the enclosure strong enough to withstand any explosion inside it and by limiting the gaps between joints of the case and of clearances for shafts, etc. As the details vary according to the gas likely to be encountered, apparatus flameproof in one gas is not necessarily flameproof in another.

The letters F.L.P. within the outline of a crown indicates that an apparatus is identical to one which has been tested by the Buxton testing station of the Ministry of Fuel and Power. The group of gases for which the apparatus has been tested is also shown. Group I comprises fire-damp; Group II includes petroleum and acetone vapours; Group III, coal gas and coke-oven gas. Group IV comprises acetylene, carbon disulphide and hydrogen, but it is impracticable to make flameproof apparatus for this, the most hazardous group, because the gaps would need to be so fine. The Ministry of Technology now administers the British Approvals Service for Electrical Equipment in flammable atmospheres and certifies flameproof apparatus and intrinsically safe electrical equipment.

Where flammable gases or vapours are liable to be present such certified flameproof apparatus should be used. There are, however, two alternatives which may be applied in appropriate circumstances—

Pressurized apparatus. Inert gas within the case of the apparatus is maintained at a higher pressure than the atmosphere outside it, so that it is not possible for gases or vapours to enter the enclosure.

Intrinsically safe equipment may be used for some purposes, such as telephone and instrument control circuits. The equipment is designed to limit the energy in the circuit that enters the area of possible danger so that any spark that could be produced would be too weak to ignite the gas or vapour for which the equipment had been certified.

CHAPTER XV

CENTRAL HEATING SYSTEMS

THE methods of central heating in use to-day include: (1) low-pressure hot-water, (2) high-pressure hot-water, (3) steam, (4) hot air.

In each case the medium employed is heated at a furnace or boiler, and, in each method except that of hot air, piping is provided to convey the medium throughout the building. Provided the heating apparatus is situated outside the building or in a fire resisting compartment, the fire hazards depend on the temperature which it is possible for the piping to attain. It will be remembered in this connection that if woodwork is subjected over a period to temperatures exceeding 300° F. (148·9° C.) the wood is liable to change its nature. Other substances, too, such as fluff, dust, and waste generally, may come into contact with the pipes and quite apart from the possibility of spontaneous combustion such materials become excessively dry and are therefore easily ignited.

The insurance offices describe as *"low-pressure"* a system in which water or steam enters the pipes at a temperature below 300° F. (148·9° C.) or at a gauge pressure of 53 lb. per sq. in. (which implies this temperature). Installations which do not conform to this limitation are defined as *"high-pressure"*.

The hazards of the various fuels capable of being used in any system are described in Chapter XVIII.

LOW-PRESSURE HOT-WATER APPARATUS

The water is heated in a boiler (placed at the lowest part of the building) to which iron piping about 2 in. to 4 in. in diameter is connected to form a system through which the water circulates, and which includes radiators to provide heating surface to warm the various rooms. The flow of water is maintained because hot water has a specific gravity less than that of cold water. When the water in the boiler is heated it rises through the "flow" pipe to the radiators, where it loses heat and is carried back to the boiler by the "return pipe." In some systems the circulation is maintained or assisted by pumps, in which event it is possible to use smaller pipes and the boiler need not be situated at the lowest part of the building. Water lost by evaporation is made up from a feed tank which is supplied with water from the mains by a ball valve.

The system must be open to the air at some point in order that the pressure cannot exceed that due solely to the height of the water in the system. The "free blow-off" is generally provided in the form of an "expansion pipe" which is open-ended and terminates over the cold-water feed tank.

The importance of the system being open to the atmosphere is contained in the fact that at atmospheric pressure the boiling point of water is 212° F. (100° C.) and this temperature cannot be exceeded. If, however, the water is subjected to additional pressure it will not boil until a higher temperature is reached. The reading on the pressure gauge of a boiler represents this additional pressure and ignores the normal pressure of the atmosphere (14·7 lb. per sq. in.). When the gauge reads 15 lb. the boiling point is 250° F. (121° C.), at 75 lb. it is 320° F. (160° C.) and so on. Provided then that the system is open to the atmosphere the only pressure, additional to that of the atmosphere, on the water in the boiler is that imposed by the height of water in the system. As each foot of height gives a pressure of 0·433 lb. it would be necessary for this to be 120 ft. to enable the temperature to reach 300° F. (148·9° C.). Although the temperature of the water pipes is thus limited care should be taken that paper, fluff, and waste are not allowed to accumulate behind pipes and radiators as they would become very dry, in which state they could easily be ignited by ordinary sources of ignition.

Situation and installation of the boiler. The boiler should be in a separate compartment, preferably a fire-resisting one. When it is installed without any enclosure it is possible for stock to be stacked near the boiler or for waste to come into contact with it.

The hazards are similar to those of steam boilers, set out on pages 115–7. The installation of appliances burning solid fuel or oil is described in Chapter XII and of gas burning appliances in Chapter XIII.

HIGH-PRESSURE HOT-WATER APPARATUS

The system comprises one continuous circuit consisting of small bore wrought-iron piping (external diameter $1\frac{5}{16}$ in.) extending throughout the building and at one point coiled around an enclosed furnace. An expansion chamber is fitted at the top of the system. The piping is filled with water, the expansion chamber with air, and the whole hermetically sealed. When the furnace is lighted the water in the coils passing around it becomes heated and circulation proceeds in a similar manner to that in a low-pressure apparatus. At the same time, however, the water expands because of the heat and, endeavouring to flow into the expansion chamber, compresses the air which is there. The compressed air exerts a pressure on the water: the hotter the water becomes, the more it expands, the more it compresses the air and therefore the greater the pressure which is imposed by the air on the water.

As the water is under pressure its boiling point is not 212° F. (100° C.) but some higher temperature. These systems usually maintain a temperature of about 300° F. (148·9° C.), but they can, if required, heat the water to higher temperatures.

The precautions required in respect of the installation of the furnace are similar to those for low-pressure hot-water boilers. Owing to the high temperature of the pipes it is important that they are kept clear of woodwork and other combustible material.

Medium pressure hot water installations are similar in hazards and construction to high-pressure hot-water apparatus. The difference is that the system is sealed not hermetically but by a heavily loaded valve. If the temperature of the water entering the pipes exceeds 300° F. (148·9° C.) they are regarded by Fire Offices as "high-pressure."

STEAM HEATING

The appearance of a steam heating system is similar to that of a low-pressure hot-water system, but the pipes contain steam instead of hot water. The boiler must, of course, differ because in a hot-water plant it is not intended to boil the water, whereas in a steam system the water must boil continuously or there would be no steam. The boiler, instead of being filled with water, is only partly filled, the upper part of the shell forming a steam dome. Owing to the higher temperature produced at the boiler it is very desirable that it should be in a fire-resisting compartment or else outside the main building. The hazards of steam boilers are described under "Power" on pages 115–7.

Steam for heating can be supplied by a boiler used only for the purpose, or by using a reducing valve from a boiler which provides steam for power purposes. Another method is to utilize "exhaust" steam, i.e. steam which has already been employed to drive a steam engine.

The temperature of the piping depends on the pressure at which the steam enters it. At a gauge pressure per sq. in. of 15 lb. the temperature is 250° F. or 121° C., and at 75 lb. it is approximately 320° F. or 160° C. The London Building Act requires steam pipes (other than those forming part of a system having a free "blow-off") to be at least 6 in. clear of combustible material irrespective of the temperature of the pipes. The Fire Offices do not prescribe any distance, as this must, for safety, vary with the temperature of the piping, but generally no objection is raised to the pressures up to 20-25 lb. per sq. in. usually employed, provided the pipes are 2 in. or 3 in. clear of woodwork. The Fire Offices do, however, discriminate in their ratings between low-pressure installations in which the steam enters the pipes at a temperature of less than 300° F. (148·9° C.) or at a gauge pressure of 53 lb. per sq. in., and those in which steam at a higher temperature is employed.

UNIT HEATERS

These are a fairly modern introduction used in place of or in addition to radiators. They consist of a metal casing containing an electric fan and a coil of piping heated by either steam or hot water. The fan draws air around the hot coils and distributes it in the direction desired. In some types steam both drives the fan and heats the air. Similar appliances are heated by gas or electricity, suitable elements taking the place of the coils. The units are generally secured to roof trusses, and provided they are permanently secured in positions where no combustible material (e.g. roof lining) is endangered they form a suitable method of heating and are out of the way of floor waste, etc.

HOT-AIR INSTALLATIONS

These types of heating apparatus incorporate a method of warming air by passing it over a heated surface and of distributing it to the rooms required to be warmed. They vary considerably in fire hazard according to the method of heating adopted: there is little comparison between modern steam heated air conditioning plants and the fire heated types which preceded them. Generally, however, the use of the term "hot air installation" is intended to imply that the source of heat is a fire heated furnace. When steam coils are utilized it is more usual to refer to "steam heated air."

Fire-heated hot-air plants. The simplest arrangement consists of a coal or coke fired stove enclosed in a casing of cast iron rather larger than the stove. Air in the space between the stove and the casing becomes warmed and as it passes out to mix with the air of the room fresh air flows in to take its place, thus providing a continuous supply of warm air. The stove itself has a flue pipe to carry away the products of combustion and to prevent them mixing with the air utilized for heating the room.

A similar plant can be used for heating several rooms or a hall by placing it in the basement. Fuel is burned in an inner case and air is warmed by flowing between the inner and outer cases. From this space the heated air is carried by ducts to the various rooms, to which it is admitted by regulators. There are also larger plants, in some of which the air is heated by passing through a number of tubes set in the firebox. The hot air is distributed throughout the building through ducts either by reliance on the fact that heated air rises or more generally by the use of power driven fans.

These plants are unpopular with insurance companies, partly because with age the furnaces deteriorate. Fires have been caused by sparks from the fire box finding their way to the air ducts via cracks or holes in the air heating tubes or the jacket surrounding the stove, and thence to the rooms of the building.

Fire hazards. The hazards of the furnaces are similar to those of boilers, described on pages 115–7. The pipes and ducts conveying the heated air throughout the building may become very hot and should not be within 6 in. of any combustible material.

Gas- or oil-heated hot-air plants. When gas or oil burners are used in place of fire heat in the furnace there is less risk of sparks being transmitted to the air ducts, but the other hazards mentioned above exist.

Steam-heated air plants utilize steam coils, around and about which air is forced by power driven fans before distribution through ducts. Often air washing and conditioning plant is incorporated. These plants do not have the hazards of fire heated plants, but it is important that the boiler necessary to provide the steam is safely located, and that the hot air ducts are fixed a safe distance from combustible materials.

The hazards of ventilating ducts which, of course, apply also to these hot-air ducts, are described in Chapter XVI.

VENTILATION—DRYING—FURNACES AND OVENS

VENTILATION is the process by which stale air in buildings is removed and replaced by fresh air. A comfortable, pure atmosphere promotes health; impurities, which arise from the breathing of persons in the room, from manufacturing processes, gas jets, etc., should be removed by changing the air sufficiently frequently—perhaps six times an hour is adequate.

Natural ventilation. If openings are provided near the floor of a room, air enters, becomes warmed by the heat of the room, rises and passes away through openings at the top of the room. Doors, windows, skylights, lantern lights, and chimneys may provide such openings or specially designed roof ventilators may be installed. Natural ventilation is often satisfactory, but in large workshops it is usually necessary to provide mechanical ventilation by the use of fans, generally, but not necessarily, driven by electric motors.

Mechanical ventilation. Before describing the systems it should be pointed out that although a room may be adequately ventilated in the sense that vitiated air is replaced by fresh air, yet some portions may seem to be oppressive owing to the lack of air movement. This defect can often be rectified by the introduction of *air circulating fans* of various types which do not change the air but relieve discomfort by circulating it.

Mechanical systems are of three kinds, known as extraction, plenum, and a combination of extraction and plenum.

Extraction system. Vitiated air is drawn out by fans and fresh air enters at points remote from the fans. This system does not permit such control of atmospheric conditions as a plenum system does, but is effective in narrow rooms. The extraction fans can be fitted in one side wall and fresh air inlets provided in the opposite side situated behind radiators or steam pipes in order that the incoming air may be warmed as it enters. Fans may discharge direct to the open or ducts may be provided. When the fans are near floor level the air inlets should be at a height of 8–10 ft., but when the fans are elevated the inlets should be 3–4 ft. from the floor.

Plenum system.—Fans force fresh air into the room and the vitiated air is allowed to escape through doors, windows, and other outlets. This system is suitable for any premises and is especially valuable in very large rooms where an extraction system cannot easily be applied. Because the slight positive air pressure in the room prevents leakage, cold draughts can be eliminated and the incoming air can be heated, cooled, or humidified as desired.

Plenum combined with extraction system. Fans are provided both for forcing fresh air into the room and for extracting vitiated air. A thorough changing of air in every portion of a building can be achieved by careful arrangement of the inlets and outlets.

Plants of this kind generally provide for *air conditioning* by means of which air is washed and humidified in a "mist" chamber containing a number of water sprayers, after which free water is removed. The air then passes through cooling or heating chambers as the case may be, and is delivered through ducts to the rooms to be ventilated, whence it is removed by other ducts.

Fire hazards. The importance of immediately closing down ventilating plant when a fire is discovered cannot be over-stressed, as such a supply of fresh air would enable a fire to extend rapidly. On the other hand, ventilation intelligently carried out by those in charge of fire fighting operations is a most important aid because smoke, heat, and gases can be removed and firemen enabled to advance to the seat of the fire. Nor should it be forgotten that ventilation reduces the risk of a fire starting in many trades and processes, particularly where flammable gases, vapours, or dust are likely to be present.

Ducts should be constructed preferably of brick or concrete but metal is often employed. Any insulating linings should be non-combustible. The use of wood ducting is objectionable. Each point where a wall or floor is pierced is a weakness and, as a fire can spread rapidly throughout a building by way of the ducts, shutters held open by fusible links should be fitted at each inlet and outlet and at the junction of a branch with a main duct. Trunks conveying heated air should not be installed within 6 in. of combustible materials.

As it is possible for sparks to be drawn into the building through the fresh air inlets they should be protected with suitable guards and their position carefully chosen. The system should not discharge into a roof space but should vent to the open.

Localized exhaust ventilation. In certain situations the standard of ventilation required is much higher than that adequate for general ventilation, e.g. in a cellulose spraying room. This is achieved by partitioning off the compartment and providing additional extraction fans. In such places fans should discharge directly to the open or, if a trunk is unavoidable, it should be as short as possible and the fan placed at the exhaust end of the trunk.

Systems for the removal of vapours, dust, and waste from woodworking machinery and from other processes, although no ventilating systems, may now conveniently be mentioned. The ducts employed are as liable to spread fires from one part of a building to another as are ventilating ducts, and if the dust conveyed is a combustible one there is the added possibility of explosion or fire in the trunks—caused perhaps by an overheated fan bearing or a spark struck by a fan: the use of non-ferrous fans obviates the latter possibility. The collecting room or cyclone should be outside the building, and if canvas or fabric bags are used inquiry should be made whether the particular dust is liable to give rise to charges of static electricity on the bags or whether particles of the dust clinging to the fabric are liable to spontaneous combustion. Both ducts and collectors should be frequently cleaned out. (See Dust Explosions, Chapter IX.)

DRYING

Such a multitude of articles in so many different trades require to be dried that it is not possible to describe in detail the various methods employed. Generally, however, there is one factor in common, that the surplus moisture is absorbed by air. The higher the temperature of air the greater the amount of water it will absorb but as there is a limit to the percentage of water that even hot air will hold, it is necessary to replace the air as soon as it is saturated by further supplies of dry air. Thus the most effective method of drying is by a current of hot air and it is in the means employed to provide this that drying systems differ.

Natural drying consists of laying out the articles to be dried either in the open air or in a situation where there is a natural draught, e.g. timber is seasoned by stacking in such a manner that air can circulate all around it.

Artificial drying usually takes place in a compartment sometimes spoken of as a kiln, and the degree of hazard depends on the combination of three factors—

1. *The combustibility of the articles or material being dried.* Obviously stricter precautions are required with textile articles or timber than with bricks or pottery. Any combustible material is more hazardous after drying.

2. *The construction of the drying compartment.* Where practicable the compartment should be fire-resisting and not communicate with the main premises otherwise than by a fire-resisting door. Any timber or other combustible material which enters into the construction of the compartment, whether floors, roofs, racks, or in any other form, becomes very dry, in which state it could easily be ignited and burn rapidly. The hazard extends to woodwork and combustible material in the proximity of the drying room to a distance dependent on the temperature.

3. *The means by which the compartment is heated.* The least hazardous methods are low-pressure hot water and low-pressure steam, either by piping fixed in the compartment or in the form of coils placed outside the compartment and over which air is blown by fans. The temperature which can be achieved by these methods is limited, and where higher temperatures are required high pressure hot water or steam pipes, gas burners, oil fired burners, stove heated air or coke stoves are often used. These forms of heating are described in other chapters. Unless the materials being dried are non-combustible it is more hazardous for the source of heat to be in the compartment, even when adequate arrangements are made to keep the materials well clear of the source of heat, than for air heated at a separate apparatus to be blown into the room by fans, but in any event the higher the temperature the greater the hazards.

Conveyor dryers are ovens or tunnels through which materials to be dried pass on continuous conveyors. Accidental stoppage of the conveyor will expose the material to heat for longer than was intended and may result in its ignition.

"Moist air kilns" for drying or seasoning timber maintain within the kiln a moist atmosphere by means of steam sprays. This method not only enables the conditioning of the timber to be expedited but very materially reduces the fire hazard.

Drying over boiler. A drying room built over a boiler room to utilize the waste heat from the boiler should have a fire resisting floor. A perforated floor, especially one of combustible construction, is unsatisfactory. No drying should be done in a boiler room itself.

Grain-drying plants usually consist of a coke- or oil-fired furnace in which air is heated and is then drawn by fan into a metal cylinder through which grain slowly falls to the bottom, where it is cooled and then sacked off. The main hazards of the dryer itself are that the air passed through the grain may be too hot or may carry with it sparks, the crops may inadvertently come into contact with the furnace or the grain may still be hot when it is bagged off. A more serious hazard, however, is the introduction of such a plant, incorporating an oil- or coke-fired furnace, into farm buildings which are often of non-standard construction and filled with combustible materials.

The Fire Offices' recommendations include that the plant, or at least the furnace, be in a separate compartment, that the dryer be of metal construction, that baffles be supplied to prevent sparks from entering the dryer, that temperature indicators be kept in good condition, that the plant be not left unattended when in operation, that cleanliness be observed at all times and that first-aid fire appliances be provided. The usual precautions described in other chapters should be taken in respect of electrical equipment, flues, coke or oil firing, and engines.

Grass-drying plants are similar in principle to grain dryers but the fire hazard is much greater; grain is not very easy to ignite but dried grass is flammable. After drying, the grass is ground to powder, introducing the additional hazard of flammable dust and the possibility of explosion. The plant should be cleared of dust and grass after each period of use.

Other methods of drying include—for materials suitable for each type—heating in pans or drums or conveying materials over steam-heated cylinders. So many small fires are caused by drying articles in front of an open fire or around a stove that it is worth noting that many of them could have been prevented by the simple precaution of using a suitable wire guard.

Gas-heated Ovens and Stoves

Apart from the general hazards of drying plants mentioned previously there is the risk in gas ovens of accumulations of unburnt gas which may subsequently be ignited and explode. To avoid this two automatic devices should be used—

(1) A flame-failure device or automatic pilot which ensures that if the flame of the burners is extinguished by any means the gas supply is cut off and cannot again flow until there is a flame at or sufficiently near to the burner to ignite the gas.

(2) A low-pressure cut-off valve which stops the gas supply if the pressure falls below that which will maintain a flame and does not permit gas to flow again until the valve is opened by hand, which cannot be done until the burner cocks have been closed.

Ventilation must be provided to supply sufficient fresh air for the burners to function and to remove the products of combustion and any flammable vapours. To prevent extinction of the burners due to lack of air the flue must be of adequate size, any dampers so arranged that the flue cannot be more than two-thirds obstructed and, to prevent down draughts, the flue should terminate a few feet above the stove, under a hood connected to a flue which passes to the open air.

Ovens should be raised at least 1 in. above floor level to allow access of air and by relieving the pressure of air to prevent the burners being blown out by sudden closing of the doors. If the floor is combustible the oven should stand on a substantial stone or concrete base.

When the material to be heated is combustible a false bottom should be fixed well above the burners so that material cannot fall on to them. Care should be taken that no waste matter liable to spontaneous ignition, e.g. oily cleaning rags, is carelessly left or deposited in the oven.

When the articles being dried give off a flammable vapour, e.g. in *enamelling ovens*, the gas burners should preferably not be in the oven itself—the working chamber—but should be in a separate compartment so arranged that the products of combustion do not pass through the working chamber but around it. In addition to the flue carrying away the products of combustion from the combustion chamber there must be another to vent the working chamber and lead the vapour from the articles there to the open and away from possible sources of ignition. Flammable deposits, e.g. paint drippings, must not be allowed to collect in the oven and painted articles should not be placed in the oven until they are sufficiently dry that no drips will fall from them.

The ovens mentioned above are known as *box ovens* and are ventilated by natural draught. Larger types of oven, either of the box type or those through which articles are continuously passing, i.e. *conveyor ovens*, are mechanically ventilated. Some, in order to reduce heat losses, re-circulate air which has already been through the oven. In such cases it is necessary to ensure that most of the flammable solvent vapours are removed in a pre-heating chamber fitted with mechanical ventilation before entering the oven or that an adequate proportion of the vapour-laden air is discharged to the open by a separate fan and replaced by fresh air in order to avoid dangerous concentrations of vapour. The gas supply should be interlocked with the ventilating system so that it is automatically stopped if the ventilation fans fail, and can be renewed only by manual means.

In all gas ovens explosion-relief vents should be fitted and the system should be well understood by the operatives.

RADIANT HEAT

Drying by radiant heat, or "infra-red rays," particularly of painted metal articles, is becoming more common because of the speed and convenience with which drying is effected.

By electricity. Electric screw-in lamps, similar in appearance to ordinary gasfilled lamps, are set in reflectors so arranged that the rays are concentrated on the surface to be dried. Usually the articles are placed on a slow-moving conveyor which passes through a "tunnel" commonly taking the form of an open frame-work supporting the lamps.

Attention should be given primarily to the ordinary hazards of the electrical equipment. Owing to the loss of efficiency which would result, it is not practicable to protect the lamps with glass globes and the method is therefore not suitable for use with cellulose paints. Where flammable vapours are given off as in the drying of synthetic and other paints or finishes with low-flash-point solvents, the apparatus should be in a spacious room or thorough ventilation provided and it is an advantage if a metal hood be placed over the apparatus to collect vapours and vent them to the open. In order to remove the bulk of the paint solvents, before the articles reach the drying tunnel they should pass through a ventilating tunnel having an exhaust system. Other precautions require care that the articles cannot be displaced from the conveyor and, in falling, break the lamps; that the risk of articles becoming overheated is guarded against; that the spraying or dipping process is well separated from the drying plant, and that paint drips, etc., are frequently removed.

By gas. The most usual type consists of a metal tunnel constructed with double walls, the gas burners being placed between the inner and the outer walls and so positioned that the inner wall is heated to about 600° F. (316° C.), becoming a "black emitter", i.e. there is no visible heat. This bears a similarity to the gas-heated enamelling ovens previously described and owing to its more robust nature and the fact that the gas burners can be well separated from the drying chamber it has advantages over the electric types.

FURNACES

The fire hazards of furnaces are similar to those of drying ovens, but as higher temperatures are attained more care is required in the location of the furnace and its flue. The exact distance from woodwork for safety depends on the size and temperature of the furnace, but 4 ft. might be regarded as a reasonable minimum in many cases. Owing to the high temperature of the gases from the flue it is essential that these are not allowed to impinge on woodwork as, for example, would be the case were the flue to terminate short of the roof. When solid fuel is used, sparks are liable to be emitted and to lodge in the roof. The hazards and precautions in connection with gas furnaces are similar to those for gas stoves.

In some types of furnace, e.g. for certain heat treatments of metals, air must be excluded and it is replaced by hydrogen or other flammable gas. Care must be taken to avoid the accumulation of mixtures of flammable gas and air in the furnace, particularly when lighting up and closing down. This can be prevented by "purging" with an inert gas, e.g. nitrogen.

CHAPTER XVII

POWER

BEFORE considering individual sources of power it is desirable to understand why the introduction of any form of power into a workshop implies increased risk. In the first place the output of the factory is increased, and if the kind of work done is liable to cause fires, more work done means more hazard. More waste is made and there are greater quantities of materials passing through the factory, increasing the intensity of any fire which may occur. These points have been considered more fully under the heading of "size," but an even more important factor is the risk arising from friction either at "bearings," which may be defined as the supports of moving parts of machines, or elsewhere.

FRICTION

Where two bodies rub on each other there is a force known as friction where the rubbing occurs which resists motion and manifests itself as heat. The practice of insurance abounds with examples of penalties, in the form of additional rates, imposed on account of hazards arising from friction.

The following are instances of circumstances in which the underlying reason for an additional charge is frictional hazard, although the penalty is not specifically imposed as such: in respect of disintegrators or grinding machines, where there are the risks of overheated bearings due to the high speed of operation, of heat generated by the grinding process, and of frictional sparks caused by hard bodies accidentally finding their way into the machine; in the case of vertical main shafting, where considerable heat is generated at the point where horizontal shafts are taken off by means of bevel wheels, and sparking frequently occurs; in the case of millstones, where pressure increases friction, and numerous other cases in different branches of industry.

The higher the speed of a particular machine the greater the friction and therefore the heat generated, but in comparing different types of machine the size of the surface over which the rubbing occurs and the class of work being done must also be considered, e.g. although a sewing machine works at a very high speed the work is very light and the friction negligible compared with a disintegrator, which may work at a slower speed but has far greater stresses imposed on it. Fortunately, from a fire viewpoint, friction results in a loss of efficiency and the engineer is, for this reason, anxious to avoid it as much as practicable. He therefore employs lubricants, which are introduced between the moving surfaces in order to reduce the friction and thus prevent overheating.

LUBRICATION

Solid lubricants, such as graphite, are sometimes used, but by far the most common are liquid or semi-liquid, consisting of hydrocarbon (mineral) oils or mixtures of mineral and vegetable or animal oils. The object is to prevent the surfaces from working in contact with each other by the interposition of an unbroken film of liquid, the particles of which move more easily, thus replacing friction between the moving parts by the very much smaller fluid friction between the particles of the liquid. Efficient means of application must be provided, for which purpose mechanical contrivances called lubricators are used. As, however, regular filling and attention are necessary the mechanic, too, must play his part; any omission may not be observed by the engineer until it is forced upon his attention by evidence of overheating. Many fires have been caused by overheated bearings.

Lubricating oils should be stored in an outbuilding and only sufficient for one day's use brought into the main buildings.

TRANSMISSION OF POWER

Where electric motors are employed it is possible, and desirable, to supply a separate motor to each machine, thus reducing transmission risks, but where a number of machines are driven from one motor, or other power unit, it is necessary to transmit the power from the motor or engine to the machines it drives. The most usual method is to employ a combination of horizontal shafts and belts, the shafts being rotated by means of a belt taken from a pulley or flywheel on the motor or engine, and belts taken from the rotating shafting as required to drive each machine. The shafting may be "overhead," where it is always visible and easily accessible, or it may be "underground," running in pits beneath the floor, usually and preferably of concrete, but sometimes of wood. There are several objections to underground shafting, the most important being that, owing to difficulty of access while machinery is running, lubrication may be neglected or done hurriedly and inefficiently; that floor waste is liable to collect in the pits, and that dust, e.g. sawdust, may collect on bearings, becoming caked with oil and ripe to ignite in the event of the bearing overheating. In the case of overhead shafting metal trays should be hung below bearings to catch oil drippings, and the bearings regularly cleaned of combustible dust or fluff. A combination of overhead shafting and a wood ceiling or wood-lined roof is a poor one, as such light woodwork is easily ignited and any oil splashings assist the combustion. Where the drive is by means of vertical shafting and the bevel gears are enclosed in wooden boxes there is the possibility of the oil-soaked wood and any light waste matter which may have accumulated in the box being ignited.

Whatever form of power transmission be used the hazard arising from friction exists, especially if the shafting is not well hung, and the more machines that are driven from one unit, the more points there are at which trouble may occur. Floor and wall openings necessary to convey the power throughout the building should be kept as small and few as possible, and the belt drives enclosed with non-combustible material. Where the main drive is by rope race, this should be separated from the building by brick walls, the necessary openings being as small as practicable.

GENERATION OF POWER

The generation of power implies the initiation of motion. Whether the motion be rotary, as in the case of an electric motor, or reciprocating (i.e. backwards and forwards), as with internal combustion engines, is of small importance, because one form can easily be converted to the other.

Methods of power generation can be considered in four main classes: (1) Wind and water; (2) steam engines and boilers; (3) internal combustion engines; (4) electric motors.

WIND AND WATER

There are in England a few instances of windmills still operating, the oldest working mill being at Outwood in Surrey; and pumps operated by windmill may be seen on the Norfolk Broads, but the lack of regular winds precludes their general use. Water mills are found more often, but in these days of cheap power it is doubtful how long they will remain. Both wind and water mills have transmission and friction risks, but clearly there is no hazard from the source of power.

STEAM ENGINES AND BOILERS

Boilers. The function of a boiler is to evaporate water into steam which collects in the top of the boiler, thence passing through pipes to an engine or other plant. Should the steam be further heated, not in the presence of water, but in a superheater usually set in the upper part of the boiler, it is known as super-heated steam.

The temperature of steam is related to its pressure. High-pressure steam has a higher temperature than low-pressure steam, e.g. at a pressure of 5 lb. per sq. in. it is 227° F. (108° C.); at 75 lb., 320° F. (160° C.). Very high temperatures may be attained, as in electricity generating stations, where the steam for turbo-generators may be as high as 1000° F. (538° C.). At such temperatures the ignition of woodwork or other combustible material in contact with, or even near to the steam pipes might be expected, and fires have been caused by the contact of insulating or lubricating oils with such pipes.

Vertical boilers are used for driving small engines and cranes, or for heating tanks or presses. They are not set in brickwork and must, therefore, be lagged to conserve the heat. The firing place is at the bottom and the heat and flames pass through a vertical flue to a metal smoke pipe.

Horizontal boilers are generally larger than vertical ones, and are set in brickwork, which encloses both sides, leaving only the crown to be lagged with asbestos or slag wool. The firing place is at one end and the flames and heat pass through a horizontal flue or flues to a brick chimney at the other end, the flues or fire tubes being surrounded by water, which is thus evaporated to steam. A *fire tube boiler* has a number of flues or fire tubes. In a *water tube boiler* the water is contained in steel tubes which pass over and through the furnace, instead of the fire tubes passing through the water.

Sometimes the water for feeding the boiler flows through a series of pipes situated between the boiler and the chimney, in order that heat which would otherwise be wasted may warm the feed water. This device is known as an *Economizer*.

Hazards. Apart from explosion, which should be guarded against by the provision of pressure gauges and two safety valves (one beyond the control of the attendant), and by regular inspections, the fire hazards are due more to the location of the boiler than to any danger in the boiler itself. Undoubtedly, the best place is in a separate building, preferably a fire-resisting shed, or, failing this, in a fire-resisting compartment in a corner of the main building, having a fire resisting door to any opening to the building.

The worst arrangement is for the boiler to be in the middle of the factory, not partitioned off in any way, surrounded with fuel, and probably waste, waiting to be burned. In such a situation a small fire, of little moment in a properly constructed boiler house, might speedily involve the whole factory, and while any enclosure of non-combustible material is better than none, inasmuch as a fire is more or less shut off from flammable material, a timber compartment, such as is often found in old buildings, is more a hazard than a help.

The flooring in front of the firing place should be of brick, stone, or concrete in order that any glowing embers which fall from the furnace shall do no damage, and it is desirable that the whole floor of the boiler house be so constructed to avoid the possibility of hot ashes, withdrawn from the furnace, being placed on a combustible floor. Vertical boilers are the chief offenders in this respect, as they are often installed in a building not originally intended to house power plant, and are placed in any odd corner; in such a case great care should be taken that wood flooring under the boiler is covered with stone at least 6 in. thick, or equivalent protection provided. The withdrawn ashes should be damped, placed in a metal receptacle, e.g. wheelbarrow, and removed outside to a properly constructed pit or bin away from combustible material. A vertical boiler usually has a metal smoke pipe, which should be carried to the open by the shortest route, care being taken to cut away combustible materials, say 6 in. from the pipe; while a brick flue is an improvement it should not be carried through the building further than necessary. There must be no timber in the flue or in the boiler setting, and any woodwork, whatever, over the boiler, e.g. a wooden floor or timber-framed or lined roof is a weakness, particularly if the room is not a lofty one.

Sometimes drying of trade materials or of workmen's clothing is effected by placing them on the crown of the boiler, but this is a practice which cannot in any circumstances be countenanced. For other forms of drying see pages 108–12.

Mechanical stokers of many different types are employed for supplying coal to large boilers, and where there is a steady demand for steam better results are obtained than by hand stoking. They have a little bearing on the fire risk, as the fuel can be kept further from the furnace and the boiler house clearer than where hand stoking is practised. Fuel must never be stored near enough to the boiler to be ignited by heat from the furnace. (For oil fuel and pulverized coal see Chapter XVIII.)

Steam engines. A steam engine converts the active energy stored up in the steam supplied by a boiler into mechanical work. In the nineteenth century steam engines were used for all power purposes, but they have been replaced to a great extent by oil engines or electric motors. They are now used where large powers are required, as in electricity generating stations, or where steam is needed for process heating, when boilers must be installed in any case.

Steam engines are divided into reciprocating engines and

turbines, but the term is more generally restricted to the former.

Reciprocating steam engines. In the simplest form, steam under pressure enters a cylinder through a port at one end. The steam, being under pressure, tends to expand, thus forcing a piston to the other end of the cylinder, being then discharged through an exhaust port. Steam is then introduced at the other end of the cylinder and drives the piston back—and so on.

Steam turbines differ from reciprocating engines in that the action is a rotary one. Steam is admitted at a uniform rate and drives the blades fixed on a rotor so that a smooth rotary motion is produced.

Steam is the safest form of power and, provided attention is given to the following points, no danger is to be apprehended from the engine itself. The engine should be in a separate compartment, preferably of non-combustible materials; if the walls or floor are of timber they should be protected against oil splashings by sheet metal. Steam pipes must be well clear of woodwork or other combustible materials. Metal bins should be provided for oily wipes.

INTERNAL COMBUSTION ENGINES

These differ from steam engines (in which the working agent, steam, is produced by the combustion of fuel in a boiler separately, and possibly some distance from the engine) in that the motive power is obtained by the combustion of an explosive mixture of gas and air *inside* the cylinder of the engine. It is in the method by which the air-gas mixture is supplied that differences arise between gas and oil or spirit engines, for in the case of the latter the oil or spirit must first be converted to gas.

The fire hazards common to all internal combustion engines are as follows, those peculiar to the different types being detailed under their separate headings.

1. *Unsuitable situation*. The engine should stand in a separate room or compartment, ideally of fire-resisting construction, having fire resisting doors, or, failing this, constructed of non-combustible materials, having doors to openings. Any woodwork liable to be splashed with oil should be protected with sheet metal. Sawdust is sometimes used to soak up oil drips, but this is not a good practice and sand should be substituted. Engines often stand on a raised concrete foundation, and this is to be commended as it obviates the likelihood of rags, dust, fluff, etc., collecting under the engine.

2. *Hot exhaust pipe*. As the function of the exhaust pipe is to carry away the products of combustion, it gets hot and must be kept well clear of woodwork or other combustible materials. Where the floor is of concrete the exhaust pipe may be embedded

in the floor, passing underground to the open; but where wooden flooring exists the best arrangement is for the pipe to pass through the nearest wall. The pipe should always vent into the open and not, for example, into a chimney, even a disused one, as it is possible for unburnt gases to be delivered *via* the exhaust and to accumulate in the flue.

3. *Fuel storage and supply.* The arrangements should be similar to those described in Chapter XVIII. Briefly, the object should be to store the fuel in a safe place where it would not be endangered by a fire in the engine room, and the supply system such that a fire in the engine room would not be aggravated by additional oil. Drums of oil should not be stored in the engine room.

4. *Oily rags.* Metal bins should be provided for the temporary reception of oily wipes, which should be removed or burnt daily.

The additional hazards of the various types are—

(*a*) **Gas engines** run on town gas from the public mains, but some, especially in large works, on producer gas (see Chapter XVIII, Fuel).

The rubber gas bag or reservoir which is placed between the gas mains and the engine, usually against the engine-room wall, must be protected against damage by a metal shield. It must not rub against a rough (e.g. brick) wall at the back, or the friction will, in time, cause leakage.

Supply piping should be of hard metal, and most certainly not, as is sometimes found with small plants, rubber or flexible piping.

(*b*) **Oil and spirit engines** work upon the same principle as gas engines, but operations commence one stage earlier—the oil or spirit must be vaporized, and it is this operation which brings additional hazards. Oils and spirits of all grades, from petrol to heavy fuel oil, are utilized, and the engines can conveniently be considered in three groups—

(i) Spirit engines, e.g. petrol. (ii) Medium oil engines, e.g. paraffin. (iii) Heavy oil engines, e.g. heavy petroleum.

(i) *Spirit engines.* Owing to the low flash point of the spirit adequate ventilation is necessary and there must be no naked lights in the engine room. The best situation for the fuel tank is in the base of the engine, the fuel being pumped up to the carburettor, where it is vaporized and mixed with air. In other cases the fuel tank is situated above the engine, the spirit flowing to the carburettor by gravity; where this method is employed the whole contents of the fuel tank may be discharged into the room in the event of the supply pipe becoming fractured. It is desirable, therefore, that the pipes be of metal, generally copper, that the tank be of small capacity, well secured, free from vibration or heat from the engine, and that a stop-cock be supplied immediately beneath the tank. No spirit, other than that in the feed tank, should be kept in the building, and the tank should not be filled while the engine is running. The main supply of spirit should be kept outside, either in cans stored in a metal bin in the open, or in an underground tank.

(ii) *Medium oil engines.* The hazards are similar to those of spirit engines but, as the flash point of the fuel is higher, the risks are reduced.

In the case of spirit engines the fuel is so volatile that it is vaporized by a current of cold air passing over it, but, for paraffin to be turned to vapour, heat is necessary. After the engine has been running for a short while the heat of working is sufficient to vaporize the oil. For starting, and until this stage is reached, either a "vaporizer" must be warmed by means of a blow-lamp, in which event the usual hazards of pressure lamps are introduced, with the added disadvantage that the lamp, while still alight, may be set down near some combustible material; or the engine is supplied with two feed tanks, one quite small containing petrol which is used for starting and until the engine is sufficiently warm, when the supply is changed to oil from the larger tank.

(iii) *Heavy oil engines* may be similar to medium oil engines but usually they are of a type specially designed for using heavy oil, known as compression-ignition engines or *diesel engines*, in which the air-gas mixture in the cylinder is fired, not by an electric spark or ignition tube, but by the heat of compression. No vaporizer is necessary as the oil is injected into the cylinder in the form of a spray operated by compressed air, and is first vaporized, then ignited, solely by heat generated through high compression in the cylinder. (Whenever a gas is compressed heat is generated and as the compression in the engines may be about 600 lb. per sq. in., temperatures of over 1000° F. (538° C.) are attained—sufficient to ignite the oil vapour and air mixture.) The engines are started on compressed air and therefore avoid the risks of starting up common to ordinary medium or heavy oil engines. The general precautions for internal combustion engines should be observed.

Electric Motors and Generators

The great advantage from a fire viewpoint in the use of electric motors over other forms of power is that, by their use, transmission risks can be considerably minimized. The best arrangement is for each machine to be driven by a separate motor or, failing this, for one motor to be supplied to each small group of machines, thus obviating the floor openings, long shaftings, and many bearings which would otherwise be required. From the user's point of view a breakdown of one motor throws only one machine or one group of machines out of use, whereas in factories where one large engine drives all the machinery its breakdown involves a complete stoppage of work ; also, if only a few machines are required to be run at a particular time, only the few motors actually driving them are consuming current. On the other hand, there are more points at which trouble may occur, and although in the majority of cases electric motors are the most suitable form of power, in a particular instance their appropriateness may depend on the kind of work being done.

Current from the public mains may be, and generally is, used to drive the motors, but where electric mains are not available, or for economical or other reasons are not used, electric power is generated on the premises.

Generators. By moving a conductor across the magnetic field existing between and around the poles of a magnet an electric current is generated. A generator consists essentially of a number of conductors rotating in a magnetic field, the current so generated being utilized for lighting, heating, or power purposes. The difference between a generator and a motor is that, whereas a generator converts mechanical energy into electrical energy, a motor converts electrical energy into mechanical energy. In other words the mechanical energy (e.g. from an internal combustion engine) used in driving the generator is transformed into electrical energy in the form of current, which can then be transmitted and applied to drive an electric motor, wherein the electrical energy is transformed back into mechanical energy.

The fire hazard of electrical generation falls into two parts : first, that of the generator, which is similar to that of a motor and is considered later; second, and generally the greater hazard, that of the machine supplying mechanical energy, i.e. the engine used to drive the generator. Steam or internal combustion engines are generally employed, and the precautions appropriate to whichever is used must be adopted; in all cases, the generating plant should be contained in a separate compartment, and not placed where combustible materials are present or flammable dusts can arise. Care must be taken that the main switchboard is in a dry, well-ventilated position, clear of woodwork, and so arranged that rubbish or other combustible matter cannot accumulate in its vicinity.

Small generating plants, consisting of a petrol engine driving a dynamo, are often found on farms and in connection with the lighting of country mansions. In these cases hazards frequently arise due to the plant being installed in an unsafe position and/or in the charge of an unskilled man.

Electric motors. Provided each motor is on a separate circuit, properly protected with fuses, and *is in a suitable situation*, the main hazard of the motor itself is that of excessive current flowing through its windings causing them to overheat and ignite the insulation: such an occurrence might take place if a motor were severely overloaded, or if a short circuit were caused by foreign matter entering the motor and damaging the insulating material. It is not possible to start electric motors, other than quite small ones, by simply turning on a switch, for if this were done excessive current would flow and damage the motor. The current must be applied gradually, and for this purpose starting gear is provided, embodying a set of resistance coils which are so arranged as to allow a steadily increasing current to flow through the motor as the starting handle is moved. Surplus current is absorbed by the coils and shows itself as heat, with the consequence that starters must not in any circumstances be mounted near combustible material, such as a timber partition, but should be contained in an earthed heavy metal case secured to a brick wall in a dry, well-ventilated situation.

The motor itself should be placed over a metal tray to catch any oil drippings, in a well-ventilated position where flammable gases cannot accumulate and where the motor is not exposed to risk of mechanical injury or to damage from water, steam, or oil, and its metal case should be earthed. Woodwork, or other combustible material sufficiently near to be ignited should fire occur at the motor, must be protected with non-ignitable material.

Often the motor is enclosed in a box lined with asbestos sheeting, *and provided this is so arranged that it allows adequate ventilation* the idea is a good one, preventing any floor waste being swept against the motor. Any accumulation of fluff, dust, etc., inside the box must be regularly removed, as, otherwise, it might be ignited by a spark arising at the commutator, slip rings, or elsewhere.

Where flammable vapours, gases, or dusts are liable to be present, approval should be given only to certified flameproof motors, i.e. those so designed that the enclosing case will withstand any explosion of gas within it and will prevent the transmission of sparks or flame capable of igniting gas, etc., in the surrounding atmosphere (see pages 99–100).

CHAPTER XVIII

FUELS

THE precautions necessary when boilers and furnaces are stoked with coal or coke have already been described; the coal should be stored in bunkers out of reach of heat from the furnace, and ashes withdrawn should be removed from the boiler house to a safe situation. Other solid fuels, however, are often employed from motives of economy or convenience: in sawmills, sawdust and wood chips are frequently used; in other risks, also, combustible waste may be utilized. The precautions are similar to those for coal, but greater care is necessary in storage, on account of the ease with which the fuel could be accidentally ignited. Fine dust should not be fed into furnaces by hand.

It has been appreciated for very many years that, theoretically, the ideal way of firing a furnace is to introduce the fuel and air simultaneously in an intimate mixture, and the two alternatives to coal or coke of most importance and increasing use—pulverized fuel and liquid fuel—both employ this method.

PULVERIZED FUEL

Coal dust in air forms an explosive mixture which may be thought of as equivalent to a flammable gas.

Grinding. The coal dust in the pulverizer may be ignited by overheating due to friction, caused either by breakage of an internal part of the machine, or the accidental introduction of small pieces of metal mixed with the coal when delivered. To avoid the latter risk a magnetic separator should be provided, over which the coal must pass before entering the machine. All plant should be earthed to remove charges of static electricity.

Leakage of coal dust from machines, pipes, etc. This can be avoided by care, but precautions should be taken so that in the event of leakage the air-dust mixture will not be ignited. (See Chapter IX, Dust Explosions.) The plant should be so designed that dust will not accumulate on ledges or in pockets.

Use of coal dryers. When the plant includes a machine for drying the coal before grinding, thus increasing the efficiency of the fuel, it should be separated from grinders and storage bins—preferably placed in a fire-resisting compartment. Often, however, a combined drying and grinding machine is used.

Storage. Pulverized coal is very liable to spontaneous combustion, especially if containing any sulphur; for this reason storage bins should not be situated near any source of heat, e.g. boilers, flues, hot-water or steam pipes.

The danger of unburnt dust in the furnace is similar to that of unburnt oil fuel described on the next page.

LIQUID FUEL

Liquid fuel has the advantages of ease of storage and replacement of supplies, convenience and cleanliness in use, and the fact that it gives a steady intense heat. It is used not only for steam boilers but for furnaces, ovens, and central heating boilers in factories, shops, and even private dwellings. Automatic thermostatic controls can be provided. Light oils may be used in small boilers, but the oils generally used are heavier grades known as fuel oils.

Fuel oil is the name given to those extracts of petroleum which have a flash point of not less than 150° F. (65·6° C.). The oil is burnt in the furnace in the form of a spray injected through special burners, at which the atomizing of the oil may be effected mechanically, by steam jet or by compressed air; in any of the methods the oil may be warmed before injection in order that it may flow and atomize more freely.

The hazard to be apprehended at the boiler itself is of a possible accumulation of unburnt gas in the furnace and flue, either through the burner becoming accidentally extinguished or by reason of the boiler being started with closed dampers, although the dampers should be constructed so that they can never be fully closed. These gases may be ignited by an incandescent object in the furnace, or by the boilerman applying a light before thoroughly clearing the furnace and flue of gas, i.e. by shutting off the oil and injecting steam or air. An explosion would probably result. This danger is often partially guarded against by the provision of automatic controls which shut off the fuel supply as soon as the flame is extinguished.

A greater hazard lies in the storage of the oil. It is true that, as this is of high flash point, it will (as is so often pointed out by manufacturers of oil burners) extinguish a lighted torch plunged into it, because at normal temperatures it does not give off flammable vapour. When, however, it is borne in mind that the temperature in any burning building is many times higher than the flash point of the oil so that it freely gives off flammable vapour, and that the amount stored, even for small installations, runs into several tons, it will be appreciated that a fire occurring *from whatever cause* would be greatly intensified, extended, and rendered more difficult of extinguishment by the presence of the oil.

Storage tanks. The first precaution is so to arrange the tanks that they shall not be involved in a fire and that oil cannot escape from them to add fuel to a fire. They should, wherever possible, be in the open, and a catch-pit (a sump beneath the tanks or a space around the tanks enclosed by oil-tight walls) having a capacity at least 10 per cent greater than that of the tanks should be provided. If, unfortunately, tanks are on or over a roof, the roof should be of concrete at least 5 in. thick and there should be a catch-pit. Storage tanks within buildings should be situated on the lowest floor in a well-ventilated fire-resisting tank chamber, the doorway having a fireproof door and a raised sill to form a catch pit of a capacity at least 10 per cent greater than that of the tank or tanks. They should be filled from the open air through fixed piping, should be supplied with indicators (not glass gauges) showing the depth of oil, should be electrically earthed, and provided with vapour vent-pipes, the upper end being in the open and turned down.

Oil supply. If the storage tanks are below the level of the burners it is permissible to deliver the oil, by pump, direct from tank to burners, but where the tanks are elevated a direct gravity flow is to be avoided, as, in the event of fire breaking out in the building, it might not be remembered to shut off the supply, or indeed it might not be possible to do so, with the result that the entire contents of the tanks would flow into the building and feed the fire. It is better to provide, inside the building, a small service tank from which the oil flows to the burners and which is replenished as required, preferably by hand pumping, from the storage tank. This service tank must be placed so that escaping oil cannot reach any heated surface and must have an overflow pipe leading either back to the storage tanks or to a safe place in the open to guard against overfilling.

Firevalves. The outlet pipe from any tank should be fitted with a stop valve and a fire valve, placed as close to the tank as possible —preferably within the boundary of the tank chamber or catch-pit. The valve should be automatically self-closing in the event of fire and controlled by fusible links arranged to operate at a temperature not exceeding 200° F. (93° C.), one over each firing place. Apart from the time saved by automatic fire valves, in the event of fire it may not be possible even to approach manually operated valves to cut off the oil supply.

Conversions from solid to liquid fuel. When solid fuel-burning apparatus is converted to oil-firing, care must be taken that the flues and chimney are suited to the new conditions.

POWER-GAS PRODUCERS

The use of town gas is considered in Chapter XIII. Most gas engines use town gas but in connection with large plants, especially those installed in factories where quantities of wood waste are made, it may be economical to manufacture power gas on the premises, and in some country districts where no gas mains exist there is no alternative to doing so.

When steam is blown through red-hot coal or coke, a flammable odourless gas known as water gas is produced, being a mixture of carbon monoxide and hydrogen, or, if air instead of steam be passed over the red-hot fuel, producer gas, a mixture of carbon monoxide and nitrogen, is generated. Either gas is suitable as a substitute for town gas in running gas engines, as is that obtained by using wood waste instead of coal or coke.

The plants in use fall into two main groups—

1. Suction gas producer plants, through which air and/or steam is *drawn* by the suction exerted by the engine on the first stroke of its cycle of operations. The gas is thus delivered directly to the cylinder of the engine and no gas holder is necessary.

2. Pressure gas producer plants, through which the steam and/or air is *forced* and the gas collected in a gas holder. These are larger plants intended for supplying a number of engines, and are not found so frequently as suction plants.

The fire hazards are similar in each case, and a description of the more common suction plant will serve also as a guide to the operations of pressure plants, in connection with which, however, there is an additional hazard in respect of leakage from the gas holder.

Suction gas producer plants consist of two main parts—the gas generator and the scrubber. The generator resembles in appearance a vertical boiler with a hopper on top through which the fuel is fed. Water, introduced at the bottom, turns to steam, and is drawn, with hot air, upwards through the red-hot mass of fuel. The gas so produced is drawn off at the top through a pipe leading to the scrubber, which is a vertical cylinder filled with coke kept wet by a spray of cold water. In passing through the scrubber the gas is cooled and relieved of impurities, and is then drawn into the engine *via* an expansion box. The necessary suction is provided by the running of the engine, but, as the engine cannot run until gas from the producer plant is supplied, some means must be provided of commencing the generation of gas without the aid of the engine. In starting up, the fuel in the body of the generator is lit and a fan is operated by hand to provide a draught (taking the place of the suction provided by the engine when running). At first the gas produced is not of suitable quality, and is allowed to escape through a waste pipe, which must vent to the open, but after a few minutes the gas is tested by the application of a flame to a test cock and, if satisfactory, is allowed to pass to the engine, the waste pipe being then shut off. As soon as the engine commences to work the fan may be stopped, but it must continue to run up to this moment, as otherwise the flame at the testing cock might be drawn back into the piping, causing an explosion of the gas contained in the scrubber.

These plants should be situated in the open or, if desired, under a light roof of non-combustible construction, in order that any gas leakage may be dissipated in the open air. If they must be inside a building they should be in a well-ventilated, fire-resisting compartment. The flooring and the loading platform should be non-combustible. The greatest risk probably arises when the scrubber is cleaned out, and before this is done the plant must be stopped for some hours and the fan worked to blow out through the waste pipe all gas remaining in the system. The foul coke contains an accumulation of gas and it is important that no naked light is near while it is being removed previous to filling the scrubber with fresh coke. When the plant is standing idle the waste cock should be left open, and before attempting to light the fire any residual gas must be removed by means of the blower fan.

CHAPTER XIX

SOME ELECTRICITY HAZARDS

STATIC ELECTRICITY

Every child has found by experiment that stroking a cat backwards in the dark produces two phenomena—first a crackling sound is heard and sparks are seen, second the cat protests both with its voice and with its claws. The second is of temporary interest only, but the first is of importance, inasmuch as it is the child's introduction to static electricity.

Static charges result from friction or bringing together and then separating dissimilar materials. Charges can be generated on the surface of both conducting and non-conducting substances. On a conducting substance the charge will spread rapidly over the surface, and if this is earthed at any point the charge will be quickly and safely removed. On a non-conductive substance the charge will spread slowly, if at all, and effective earthing will be more difficult as only the portion or portions in contact with the earthing device will be affected by it. Should a charge be generated more quickly than it can be discharged it will accumulate on the substance. An electrified body tends to lose its electricity by sparking towards other bodies near it, and, owing to the high temperature of an electric spark, any flammable vapours or dust clouds in the vicinity may easily be ignited.

Precautions take the following forms—

Earthing. Metal and other conducting materials should be effectively bonded, i.e. electrically interconnected, and earthed in order that the charges may be safely conducted away. This is the most usual method and is applied either alone or in addition to other methods.

Humidification of the air, thus making it sufficiently conductive to dissipate static charges.

Ionization of the air, rendering it conductive, by radioactive isotopes. The radioactive material is contained in metal cases fitted to the machines to be protected.

The following are a few examples of the different ways in which static electricity can be produced in industrial operations.

Friction of belts against pulleys, of grain against a wooden shute, or of rolls of paper against heated drums, as on paper-making machines or rotary printing machines. In these cases earthed metal combs, or copper wire can be placed in contact with the belt or paper, immediately after the place where the charge is generated. In the cases of cotton fabric, paper, etc., moving over cylinders the charges can be neutralized by passing the material through a high voltage alternating electric field, which must be so arranged that it will not itself provide a source of ignition. Care is needed in connection with photogravure (intaglio) printing machines because the inks give off flammable vapours—ample ventilation, too, must be provided.

At rubber-coating machines. Highly flammable vapours are given off: similar precautions are necessary and the air should be humidified.

In dust clouds, by friction with the air. The best safeguard is to humidify the air, as charges are not formed so readily in a damp atmosphere and are more quickly dissipated, but where this is not possible all machinery, pulleys, etc., should be earthed.

Filling of tanks with petrol from tank wagons. Charges are formed both on the tanks and on the liquids. The necessary precautions include earthing of both the tanks and wagons and the provision of a filling pipe, either entirely of metal or having an internal lining of coiled wire, in either case electrically-connected to both the wagon and the tank.

Dry cleaning. White spirit is a bad conductor of electricity, and when textiles articles are moved about in it, or rubbed with it, they become electrically charged. Should a spark be thus caused the mixture of vapour and air is likely to ignite and cause an explosion. In dry-cleaning works where white spirit is used, washing machines should be earthed and have self-closing, air-tight lids; they should be allowed to stand for several minutes after working before being opened, in order to allow the static charge to leak away to earth. The ordinary precautions adopted where flammable vapours are present—free ventilation and the avoidance of any possible source of ignition—must be observed in addition to the special precautions against static charges.

White spirit is not now used in dry-cleaning works as much as formerly. Its place has been taken largely by perchlorethylene or other non-flammable solvents. This is an example of how fire hazard can be reduced by the substitution of one material for another. At one time dry-cleaning works formed very heavy risks because benzine (highly flammable) was used and all the hazards of using and storing such liquids, including that of static electricity, were present. When benzine was replaced by white spirit (flammable) there was a reduction in hazard, and now that non-flammable solvents are employed there is an additional, even greater, reduction. Where no flammable solvents at all are used the risk of vapours being ignited by static discharges is obviously eliminated.

When dry-cleaning is undertaken at home, petrol is generally used and numerous deaths have occurred, sometimes through rubbing articles, particularly silk, and thus producing static charges, but more usually through the vapour drifting, perhaps a considerable distance, to a flame.

Lightning

In 1751 Franklin demonstrated the identity of lightning with an electric spark by tapping a thundercloud of some of its electricity by means of a kite, but in spite of this and of much more recently acquired knowledge, the behaviour of lightning is not completely comprehended.

The electricity in a thundercloud is generated by friction of warm air passing over the earth's surface and then rising, of the water vapour in the air condensing into raindrops, and of the drops breaking up into others. A difference of electrical potential is thus established in the atmosphere, either between neighbouring clouds, or between a cloud and the earth. The intervening air acts as an insulator, but, in time, the difference in potential may become so great that the air is unable to support the stress, with the result that a large spark discharge takes place in the form of one or more lightning flashes. When the discharge occurs from cloud to earth it takes the line of least resistance, and as air is a poor conductor of electricity the discharge chooses the easier method of descent by way of any better conductor that is in the vicinity. Such conductor may be a church spire, a building in a high and isolated situation, a weather vane, or other projecting object.

Lightning conductors. A lightning conductor serves a useful purpose in providing an easy path for a lightning flash, thus protecting surrounding property from damage which might otherwise occur by reason of the discharge passing through it on its way to earth. It has been suggested that a lightning conductor, by relieving the electric pressure between a cloud and the earth, serves the additional purpose of preventing a flash from occurring at all, but this is uncertain.

Rods should be of non-rusting metal, generally copper, sufficiently thick to conduct any discharge without melting, and fixed to the building vertically, projecting above the highest parts. The bottom end should be earthed to a metal plate sunk in the ground sufficiently far to be always moist, and where this is not practicable a quantity of metal should be buried with the plate; the earthing should not be near a gas main. Every portion and projection of the building must be protected; as a guide to the numbers necessary, it may be assumed that a rod will protect a cone-shaped area having its apex at the top of the rod, the radius of the circle at its base being one to two times the height of the rod.

ACCUMULATOR CHARGING

Since accumulators do not generate but merely store electricity, it follows that they require recharging at intervals when the original store has been exhausted. In the early days of radio, celluloid-cased batteries were common, but nowadays fewer batteries are used, and these, like motor vehicle batteries, have cases of materials which are not easily ignited. As the main hazard was the celluloid case, accumulator charging is now a much less hazardous process than it was.

Fire hazards. Hydrogen is given off while batteries are being charged, particularly if they are charged at too high a rate. Ample ventilation must, therefore, be provided, and care taken to avoid sparks or arcs which might ignite the gas. These can be caused by the leakage of current from one accumulator to another, by the use of corroded wiring, broken connecting wires, or loose terminals.

Precautions. The accumulators should stand in a well-ventilated situation on a non-conducting, non-porous, non-combustible surface, e.g. plate glass, glazed tiles, or slate, so spaced that they are at least 1 in. apart. Combustible material near to, or within 6 ft. above, the bench should be protected with asbestos sheeting. As much of the wiring as possible should be permanent and proper terminals supplied. Any resistances should not be near combustible material, nor where hot fragments could fall from them on to accumulators. Accumulators should not be left on charge unattended and a bucket of sand or a dry powder extinguisher should be provided.

OIL-COOLED TRANSFORMERS

High tension electric power transmission has necessitated the installation of oil-cooled transformers in many factories. Fires have occurred due to the oil becoming ignited through overheating of the transformer, and in some cases burning oil has overflowed. Such transformers should be situated outside the main buildings or in a separate fire-resisting compartment; in either case so arranged either by the provision of sumps filled with pebbles beneath the transformer or by the use of dwarf walls, that any escaping oil cannot gain access to the main buildings.

Oil-immersed switchgear. In high-pressure circuit breakers the contacts are immersed in oil to prevent an arc being maintained when the switch is operated. The hazards are similar to those of oil-cooled transformers.

Carbon dioxide or vaporizing liquids may be used for extinguishing fires in these or other oil-filled electrical apparatus. Many transformer, etc., chambers have automatic carbon dioxide installations with fixed piping; others have water spray equipment. Provided the current can be shut off, a fire may be dealt with in a similar manner to any other oil fire.

HIGH-FREQUENCY (OR RADIO-FREQUENCY) HEATING

This is a method used in the plastics and other industries by which poor conductors of heat may be conveniently and evenly heated. A valve generator produces an oscillating electric field of suitable frequency in the material being heated which is placed between two metal plates connected to the generator. The theory is that the high-frequency current transfers energy to the molecules of the material causing it to heat. The fire hazards arise from the possibility of short circuits and arcs in the event of electrical breakdown and of ignition of combustible materials undergoing heating.

COMPUTERS

A fire within a computer is likely to be of electrical origin, but the most noteworthy hazard is the large value in a small space. Any fire involving a computer, whether it originates within or outside the apparatus, will be costly. Computers, therefore, should be housed in a separate building or in a fire resisting compartment, where walls and floors and any openings in them conform to the Fire Offices' Committee Standard II Construction Rules.

ELECTRIC BLANKETS

The main causes of fire in electric blankets are overheating caused by folding or creasing, broken elements and faulty flexible leads. Many of the fires which occur every year causing death or injury could be avoided by regular inspection and testing of the blankets.

THERMOSTATS

A thermostat is a heat-operated device often used to maintain an apparatus at a constant temperature. It consists of an expansible element which automatically cuts off the current when the temperature exceeds that for which the thermostat is set. Thermostats can be valuable safeguards when they are properly maintained but they are not infallible. Failure may result from the entry of dust or fluff, deterioration through age or arcing, or the sticking of the contacts in the closed position.

CHAPTER XX

SOME MISCELLANEOUS HAZARDS

A MANUFACTURING risk is said to be "silent" when the machinery therein is not worked for manufacturing purposes. An "empty" building, of course, is devoid of all contents.

The hazards in connection with empty buildings depend largely upon the condition in which they have been left by the previous tenants. It is not unusual to find the premises littered with rubbish, trade waste, unwanted wooden fittings, and other combustible matter, which should be removed at the earliest opportunity. Any broken windows or gratings should be made secure, either by replacing glass or covering the opening with sheet metal, to prevent any malicious or careless persons from dropping or throwing in such articles as glowing cigarette-ends or lighted matches, and to obviate the possibility of sparks finding their way into the building. In rough neighbourhoods it may be desirable to protect windows against missiles with wire netting.

The premises should be securely locked to prevent the entrance of undesirable visitors; tramps frequently make use of empty buildings and, even if they do not light fires for warmth or cooking purposes, are liable to be careless in the disposal of cigarette-ends, etc. Electric and gas supplies should be shut off at the mains, but sprinkler or fire-alarm installations should be maintained in good order.

The same precautions should be taken with silent risks, but in this case the additional question of moral hazard may arise. The fact of a risk being "silent" may imply an unsuccessful business: it may be the result of bankruptcy, inability to meet financial obligations, or other unsatisfactory features. In such circumstances the buildings, plant, or stock may well be a potential liability to the owner instead of an asset, and a fire might react to his advantage by ridding him of an encumbrance.

Arrangements are often made for the occasional lighting up of boilers, etc., to keep them in good condition, and in spite of the possibility of a fire being so originated it is probably a good practice, as it indicates that the owners still take an active interest in the preservation of the property. The employment of a reliable watchman is a good general safeguard.

BUILDINGS IN COURSE OF ERECTION OR DEMOLITION

Buildings in course of erection are not, as a rule, very heavy risks, and as a night watchman is almost invariably employed, chiefly to prevent pilferage, an outbreak of fire is generally observed soon after its inception.

Concrete mixers and circular saws are driven by portable petrol engines, with the risks attendant upon the working of the engine and the storage of petrol. A quantity of shavings is made, due to the large amount of woodworking necessary, while stocks of timber, paints, etc., provide combustible material. Wooden scaffolding and staging is still employed, although it is now customary to use metal scaffolding; tarpaulins and plastic screens are often used to protect unfinished work. Temporary electric installations are used and forms of heating are required for warming bitumen, solder, etc., for the comfort of employees and the preparation of their meals. Acetylene may be used for welding, and blow-lamps for various jobs. Rubbish is burnt on or near the site.

Where structural alterations are made to an existing building some of the above described hazards exist, varying according to the nature of the alterations. The hazards are rather more serious when the building is in occupation on account of the additional combustible contents present.

The risks of buildings in course of demolition are somewhat similar to those of buildings in course of erection, but probably less care is exercised by the contractors and their workmen.

PAVEMENT LIGHTS AND GRATINGS

Cellar gratings at pavement level permit careless passers-by to drop glowing cigarette-ends or matches into the cellar. Small courts in front of cellars, sometimes known as "areas" (not to be confused with the areas mentioned in Chapter V), are often covered with pavement gratings and are liable to become depositories for rubbish. If the gratings are not required for light or air they can be covered on the underside with sheet metal; otherwise fine mesh wire netting or expanded metal should be fixed there and the space under kept clear of combustible materials. For the same reasons broken pavement lights should be repaired and cellar flaps, used for the reception of goods, kept closed when not in actual use.

REFRIGERATORS

Small refrigerating plants are being increasingly used in butchers', fishmongers', and other food shops, and in private houses, hotels, etc., while large plants are installed in many wholesale trade premises. Most small refrigerators depend on the principle that when a liquid passes into a gaseous state heat is absorbed, and those in use can be divided into two kinds: those employing compression and those relying on absorption of gas.

Fire may originate at the electric motor, or other form of power used, or by reason of the pipe leading to the condensing coils becoming so hot as to char woodwork or other combustible material in contact with it. Fire hazards may also arise from the accidental escape of the refrigerant employed, should it be either flammable, e.g. methyl chloride, or of a nature likely to hamper efforts at fire extinguishment, e.g. ammonia.

FRYING STOVES

Stoves for deep frying are used in fish-fryers' shops and in canteen and other kitchens. The pans should be fitted with close-fitting lids because if the fat ignites it is usually better to close the lid and confine the fire to the pan rather than to attempt to extinguish the fire. Hoods over the pans and ducts leading from them should be well clear of combustible material and deposits of condensed fat vapour frequently removed from them.

BANANA-RIPENING ROOMS

These are almost invariably timber-partitioned-off compartments, kept at a steady temperature of about 60° F. by means of gas jets. The burners should be enclosed with wire guards in order to prevent any loose straw used for packing from coming into contact with the flame, and should be fixed a safe distance—say 12 in.—from the timber partitions. Another method of fruit-ripening depends on the use of a weak mixture of ethylene (a flammable gas) and air—in this case care must be taken that no naked lights or other source of ignition are present. Carbon dioxide is sometimes used, but this is a non-flammable gas.

MELTING

Heat is used for melting solid substances, e.g. fats, waxes, tar, sugar, glue, etc., in a vast number of trades, and the appliances used are too numerous for individual mention. The crudest method consists of placing the substance to be melted in a vessel which is then heated by the direct application of heat from either a fire or a gas-ring. Considerable risk of boiling over arises, especially if the pan be carelessly filled above the customary level, and, if the material be of a combustible nature, its ignition is almost certain. This method is not at any time desirable, but the risks can be minimized by so securing the apparatus that it cannot be upset, by turning in the rim of the vessel to reduce the probability of boiling over and by so arranging the apparatus that any overflow cannot come into contact with the flames.

The safest method is to use steam-jacketed pans (the vessel containing the material being melted is enclosed with a "jacket" supplied with steam from the works' boiler), which not only reduce the probability of a "boil over" but avoid the danger of ignition in the event of such an occurrence. Where steam is not available water-jacketed pans are a good substitute, though arrangements must be made to prevent any overflow from coming into contact with gas-rings or other appliances used for heating the water. Wood floors under all kinds of melting appliances should be suitably protected.

INDIRECT HEAT TRANSFER SYSTEMS

Many modern processes demand heating well above the economic limit for steam and for which direct heating is unsuitable. A typical plant includes a gas- or oil-fired furnace comprising banks of tubes in which a heat transfer medium, such as "Dowtherm" or "Mobiltherm", is heated and then pumped through a ring main at a temperature as high as 700° F. (371° C.). Branches from the ring main convey the oil to each apparatus to be heated, where the temperature is controlled by the rate of flow of the heated oil. The hazards are the high temperature and the possibility of leakage of the oil, which would be emitted as a spray and easily ignited. Its flash point is around 350° F. (178° C.).

WELDING

Welding, which is the process of uniting metals by fusing them together when they are in a plastic condition brought about by heating, is practised by metal workers, motor vehicle repairers, and others. The very high temperature necessary is attained either by the use of an oxy-acetylene blow pipe flame or by electrical welding plant. Neither should be used where flammable gases, vapours, or dusts are liable to be present.

Oxy-acetylene blow pipes are used both for welding purposes and for cutting metals. It is generally appreciated that as the flame is such a hot one it must not come into contact with combustible materials, but sufficient care is not always taken to prevent hot pieces of metal and molten slag from dropping on to combustible material: when work takes place over a wood floor a tray should be placed beneath the work. Hot sparks are thrown some distance, and if there is a possibility of their alighting on ignitable matter metal screens should be used to confine such sparks.

When small quantities of the gases are required intermittently the supply is usually from cylinders, but in places where large volumes of gases are necessary an acetylene generator (see pages 87–8) is installed and possibly also a liquid oxygen plant.

Care of cylinders of gases. The risk of explosion is less when the acetylene is supplied from cylinders than when a generator is used. Cylinders of dissolved acetylene should be stored upright; they must not be kept in hot places or roughly handled. Leakage from fittings is to be avoided. Cylinders of compressed oxygen demand similar care. It should be noted that oil or grease must not be used on valves or fittings, as they are liable to ignite spontaneously in the presence of oxygen. Any leakage of oxygen would intensify a fire already burning.

Liquid oxygen plants are not found so often as acetylene generators. Even large users of oxygen generally obtain the gas in cylinders. When, however, a liquid oxygen plant is installed the precautions necessary are to avoid leakage of the gas, which would greatly assist any fire, to ensure that no oil is used on valves and that no combustible material is near the plant.

Oxy-propane blowpipes, too, are used for cutting metals. Propane is a liquefied petroleum gas usually supplied in cylinders, and the hazards of cutting are similar to those of cutting with oxy-acetylene.

Electric welding. Provided the usual electrical safeguards are observed, the only hazards arise from the possibility of flying sparks or molten metal igniting combustible materials. Metal shields should, therefore, be placed around the plant and any wood flooring adequately protected. The work must not be done where flammable atmospheres are likely.

SOLDERING AND BRAZING

In these processes the surfaces to be joined are heated (but not to such an extent as to render them plastic as in welding) and united by the application of an alloy, which adheres to, or interfuses with, the metals to be joined.

Soldering is performed with a heated iron, and the fire hazards lie in the methods employed in heating the iron. Tinmen's stoves, whether heated by gas or by solid fuel, should stand on a heavy metal tray, well above the bench, or on a 2-in. thick stone slab—a sheet metal covering to a wooden bench is not sufficient to prevent the bench becoming charred. Rests should be provided in order that the hot iron, when not in use, shall not be laid down against combustible material.

Brazing, or hard soldering as it is sometimes termed, produces a stronger joint. The parts to be joined are heated in a furnace, brazing hearth or forge, or, if small enough, by a gas blow-pipe or a blow-lamp. *Forges*, whether used for brazing or for other purposes, are usually fuelled with coke, and a draught is supplied either by bellows or by an electrically-driven fan. Care should be taken that there is no combustible matter near the forge or its flue, and a hood should be supplied to catch sparks. *Gas blow-pipes* use Town gas from the public mains, and sometimes an oxy-Town gas flame is used, in which case the oxygen is obtained from cylinders. There should be no combustible material near the work upon which the flame could impinge, and here again a sheet-metal covering is not sufficient protection to a wooden bench.

Blow-lamps burn mineral oil or spirit under pressure, when the general risks of filling and lighting up exist. They can also burn liquefied petroleum gas. A serious hazard of blow-lamps is that they are liable temporarily to be put aside while still alight, and may ignite combustible matter near which they have been placed. Blow-lamps are used not only for soldering purposes, but by painters for removing old paint, and by plumbers.

LIGHT METALS

This term includes aluminium and magnesium and their alloys, which are much used when lightness combined with strength is required.

Magnesium and its alloys (elektron is a prominent example) in the mass, such as ingots or castings, are very difficult to ignite, but when finely divided in the form of turnings, swarf, or dust they will burn fiercely. Such forms can be ignited by friction during machining or by sparks.

Precautions include keeping the machine and floor clean and dry; not allowing turnings to accumulate, but placing them in a metal bin with a lid; keeping tools very sharp and taking heavy cuts to avoid friction and the production of fine turnings; avoidance of tool grinding operations which produce sparks. The dust is especially hazardous and will form explosive mixtures with air. Grinding of magnesium or its alloys should be performed only in detached sheds and special precautions taken.

Should a fire occur, water must not be applied, as hydrogen would be liberated and the fire would be intensified. Powdered asbestos, asbestos-graphite or, less satisfactorily, dry sand should be gently applied so as to cover and smother the fire but not disturb the burning material. Small fires can often be smothered with an asbestos hand cloth.

Aluminium and its alloys can be regarded as non-hazardous, except in the form of dust clouds when precautions must be taken against ignition. A process associated with some aluminium alloys, e.g. duralumin, is of interest.

Heat treatment in nitrate salt baths. The alloys can, by heat treatment, be softened, in which state they are easy to work, but have the property of regaining hardness after a few hours. The heat treatment consists of immersing the metal in a "salt bath", a steel tank containing alkali nitrates and nitrites, heated to 400°–500° C., at which temperature the mixture is liquid.

If water or carbonaceous materials, e.g. oil, grease, rags, food, wood, get into the bath there is the probability of an explosion which would scatter molten salts over a wide area, causing ignition of oxidizable matter with which they came into contact.

Precautions include regular removal of sludge, automatic control of temperature and constant supervision by a competent, knowledgeable person. Stocks of salts should be stored away from the workroom in a dry place, as should the empty bags which are flammable due to remaining traces of nitrates.

Salt baths are occasionally used for the heat treatment of metals other than aluminium alloys.

Other combustible metals. Hafnium, Thorium, Titanium, Uranium and Zirconium may be termed combustible metals because of their relative ease of ignition and ability to support combustion. Their fire hazards are similar to, but greater than, those of magnesium.

OIL QUENCH BATHS

In the process of hardening steel the hot metal is plunged into a liquid which will cool it. When the liquid is oil, the oil sometimes becomes overheated by the rapid and continuous quenching of hot articles, and vaporized oil is ignited by a piece of hot steel. Oil quench baths should be so situated that there is no combustible material, e.g. timber roof-trusses, near them.

INCUBATORS AND BROODERS

These are used to provide the warmth necessary to hatch eggs and to rear chickens, turkeys and other livestock. The heat may be provided by oil, town gas, liquefied petroleum gas, electricity or other means, and the hazards are similar to those of other heating appliances using the same fuel.

Deep litter houses (broiler houses) for poultry, etc., raising are sheds whose floors are covered with wood chips, etc., which provide ready fuel for any fire.

MOBILE POWER-DRIVEN GOODS HANDLING APPLIANCES

In many factories and warehouses, runabout trucks are used, some being driven by electricity, but the majority by petrol engines. The fuel tank should be so fitted that it and its valves and connections are not exposed to damage, and a shut-off valve should be provided. When the fuel is liquefied petroleum gas, the fuel container should be connected to the supply pipe by a quick-disconnecting, self-closing coupling, and automatic shut-off and pressure relief valves should be installed. The induction system should include a flame arrester, and the exhaust system be arranged to prevent the discharge of flame or sparks, or of hot gases on to combustible material, and to preclude contact with combustible material. Any leakage of fuel must not be able to reach the exhaust system. There should be a master switch to disconnect the battery.

Fuel tanks should not be filled or emptied in the building and fuel should not be stored there.

In vegetable-fibre warehouses, no vehicle or appliance, unless powered only by electric batteries, should be allowed other than in a loading or unloading place of non-combustible construction.

DECORATIONS AND THEATRICAL EFFECTS

When rooms are decorated with paper hangings, carnival novelties, celluloid articles, cotton wool, and other fancy goods, fires often occur. Christmas trees and holly, too, are easily ignited when they are dry. It is obvious that candles should not be used in conjunction with such materials, but it is not always realized that electric fairy lamps, which are usually strung up on poor quality flexible cords and fittings, involve any risk. Decorations in contact with these or with ordinary lighting bulbs may be ignited, especially if the lamps are partly enclosed in, say, cotton wool so that ventilation is impeded. Such decorations may fall into open fires or on to stoves or be ignited by still-glowing discarded matches or cigarette ends.

Theatrical performances in village halls, etc., involve the use of scenic effects, flimsy draperies and dresses. A chemical extinguisher should be kept on the stage and another in the space beneath it, which is usually a store for odds and ends; a useful precaution is to provide a blanket in each dressing room. No celluloid films should be used in such halls.

RADIOACTIVE MATERIALS

The fire and explosion hazards of radioactive materials are the same as those of the materials when not radioactive. The use in industry of solid or liquid radioactive materials is fairly widespread, but the quantities are usually so small and such care is taken of them that they do not form a hazard in the ordinary sense. They may, however, increase a loss because their release by fire or during fire extinguishment may contaminate the surrounding area, and as radiation presents dangers to human beings a part of the premises may be rendered unusable until it has been decontaminated; in some circumstances this could be a difficult and costly process. As fire fighting may be delayed when firemen are aware that radioactive materials are present but do not know their location, all such areas should be plainly marked. Whenever radioactive materials are in use, it should be the duty of a designated officer to remove them to a safe place in any emergency.

CHAPTER XXI

HAZARDOUS GOODS

In estimating the fire hazards of a particular substance or class of goods, three main factors must receive consideration—

1. The risk of the goods originating a fire.
2. The risk of them spreading a fire already started.
3. Their susceptibility to damage.

1. **Originating risk** includes liability to—

  (a) Ignite and burn easily. Flammability, e.g. celluloid.

  (b) Give off flammable vapours—volatility, e.g. petrol.

  (c) Spontaneous combustion, e.g. lampblack.

  (d) Dangerous reactions in contact with water, e.g. quicklime or with other substances, e.g. nitric acid with charcoal or straw.

  (e) Explosion.

2. **Spreading and contributory risk** includes—

  (a) Spreading fires by migrating vapours or flowing liquids, e.g. petrol, oils, or melted solids, e.g. tallow.

  (b) Flammable matter generally.

  (c) Oxygen carriers, which intensify a fire, e.g. nitrates and chlorates of potash and soda.

  (d) Substances which retard extinguishment by—

    (i) Precluding the use of water, e.g. carbide of calcium, metallic powders.

    (ii) Giving off poisonous gases or noxious fumes, e.g. acids, sulphur.

3. **Susceptibility risk.** Where goods are easily damaged by smoke or water a heavy loss may result from even a small fire in a building in which they are stored, e.g. tobacco. Sometimes water damage can be avoided by the use of carbon dioxide or dry powder for extinguishment.

STORAGE

Whenever possible hazardous goods should be stored separately from those which are non-hazardous, not only to prevent a fire spreading to the latter, but also to avoid the smoke and water damage which they might sustain during a fire in the hazardous goods. Warehouses, where large values are probable, should be detached or separated by party walls from factories and workshops, where fires are more likely to start; raw materials should be stored apart from finished stocks, and where possible different classes of goods should be separated. When separate storage is not possible there are usually several rather obvious precautions to be taken, e.g. foodstuffs should not be stored where they are likely to be contaminated by poisonous vapours or noxious odours given off from other goods on fire; substances which react with one another giving off heat should be kept apart—in this category are acids and alkalis, oxygen carriers and combustible materials, and so on.

Goods should be so stacked as to permit easy access by fire-fighters, e.g. in small stacks separated by gangways and having an adequate space between the top of the stacks and the ceiling; they should be raised clear of floors to avoid water damage. Briefly, the precautions to be observed in storage are those necessary (1) to avoid the inception of a fire, and (2) to avoid a heavy loss should a fire occur.

The following notes indicate briefly the hazards of the more common hazardous goods. References are made to the pages on which the hazards are more fully considered.

Acetone. Highly flammable volatile liquid. See Chapter VIII.

Acetylene. Flammable and explosive gas. See pages 87–9.

Acids give off noxious fumes when heated and thus seriously retard fire-fightiug. Usually stored in carboys of glass or earthenware, which are liable easily to be broken, when the escaping acid itself may injure firemen or destroy, by reason of corrosive effects, goods stored near. *Chromic acid* may cause fire if in contact with combustible substances. *Sulphuric acid* (vitriol) must be kept away from chlorates and organic matter. *Nitric acid* may initiate fire if in contact with hay, straw, charcoal, or oil of turpentine. *Hydrocyanic (prussic) acid* is both flammable and very poisonous. *Picric* and *formic acids* are flammable. A general precaution for acids is to store them in a cool place in such a manner that the containers are protected from breakage, and as far as possible from organic matter and oxygen carriers.

Alcohols. Flammable liquids. See Chapter VIII.

Ammonium nitrate is a fertilizer liable to explosion as is ammonium nitrate. See oxidizing agents.

Anthracene. Coal distillation product used for making dyes. Flammable as a liquid (creosote), less hazardous as crystals.

Bags and sacks, empty but which have contained nitrates, sugar or oily, greasy or treacly material. Easily ignited and may be liable to spontaneous combustion.

Benzene (or benzole), coal tar derivative, and benzine, petroleum derivative. Flammable liquids. See Chapter VIII.

Bitumen. Easily ignited and liable to spread fire by flowing.

Bleaching powder (chloride of lime), in contact with acids or even with damp air, evolves chlorine gas—not flammable, but suffocating and liable to hamper firemen. When exposed to heat, it liberates oxygen.

Butane. Flammable gas. See pages 86–7.

Calcium carbide will not burn, but moisture, even the moisture of the air, will cause it to give off acetylene—a highly flammable gas. See pages 87–9.

Camphor is a solid substance, obtained from camphor-tree oil, used in the manufacture of celluloid and as a preventive against moths. Flammable and aids combustion of articles treated with it.

Carbon disulphide. Highly flammable, volatile and poisonous liquid. See Chapter VIII.

Cellulose nitrate is an explosive, but when stored wet or in solution in alcohol and contained in airtight drums is not regarded as within the scope of the Explosives Acts. See Chapter X.

Cellulose solutions contain cellulose nitrate and solvents which give off flammable vapours. See Chapter X.

Celluloid. Very hazardous solid. May give off explosive vapour. See Chapter X.

Charcoal. Easily ignited and liable to spontaneous combustion. See Chapter VII.

Chlorates of soda and potash. See oxidizing agents.

Coal. Liable to spontaneous combustion. See Chapter VII.

Collodion is cellulose nitrate dissolved in ether or alcohol. It is a highly flammable liquid used in photographic material factories and some artificial silk works.

Copra. Easily ignited and liable to spontaneous combustion.

Cotton. See Vegetable fibres.

Creosote. Oily distillate from coal tar or wood. Various grades. most of them flammable.

Ether. Highly flammable and volatile liquid. See Chapter VIII.

Ethyl acetate, e. butyrate, e. ether, e. lactate, etc. Flammable liquids.

Ethylene, a highly flammable gas used for fruit ripening and as an anaesthetic.

Ethylene oxide, a highly flammable gas used as a fumigant.

Explosives. Gunpowder is a mixture of saltpetre, sulphur, and charcoal. *Gun cotton* is made by treating purified cotton waste with nitric and sulphuric acids. *Nitroglycerine* is prepared by the action of a mixture of nitric and sulphuric acids upon glycerine. It is used in the form of dynamite, in which it is mixed with siliceous earth. Very many kinds of explosives are in use, but nearly all are nitro compounds, i.e. similar to gun-cotton or nitroglycerine. Great care is necessary in their manufacture, storage, and use. Most are exploded by detonation, for which purpose detonators are used. *Detonators* are almost invariably fulminate of mercury, a substance which when dry explodes if struck or heated. Fog signals, coloured fires, cartridges, etc., are all classed as explosives.

Where explosives are stored, there is the probability of an explosion should a fire occur. Apart from actual damage caused by the explosion, burning fragments may be flung considerable distances and the fire extended. Where explosives are manufactured the premises consist of small detached sheds of fragile construction, so that an explosion in one will not affect the others. Elsewhere, only small quantities should be kept.

Fancy goods are generally flimsy and flammable.

Fibres. See vegetable fibres.

Fire lighters. Clearly these are hazardous, as they are made to burn. Usually consist of wood, shavings, sawdust, or cardboard soaked in tar, mineral oils, or naphthalene. They should be stored in a detached shed or in metal bins.

Fireworks are made from gunpowder, sulphur, charcoal, and nitrate or chlorate of potash. These are all hazardous goods separately or in combination. Fireworks containing both sulphur and a chlorate are not allowed in this country. Where small quantities are kept in shops for sale in November they should be stored in metal cases. The hazards arising from carelessness in use are obvious.

French polish. Shellac dissolved in methylated spirit. Flammable.

Gases, compressed in steel cylinders. Should a fire occur where any of these are stored, an explosion may result from the excessive pressure caused by the heat, or at any time leakage may occur if the cylinders or their valves become damaged. Compressed "permanent" gases so stored include carbon monoxide, coal gas, hydrogen, methane, all of which are lighter than air: liquefied gases include ethylene (lighter than air), ethyl chloride, and methyl chloride (heavier than air). All these gases are flammable and will form explosive mixtures with air. In fires the cylinders should be kept cool by copious supplies of water at low pressure. For *acetylene* see page 87, *oxygen*, page 138, and *liquefied petroleum gases*, page 86.

Insecticides. The hazard is that of the solvent in which the chemical is disolved, e.g. white spirit, kerosene.

Lampblack. Easily ignited. Liable to spontaneous combustion. See Chapter VII.

Lime. Quicklime does not burn, but when wetted, even by rain or dew, develops great heat, sufficient to ignite easily combustible matter near it, e.g. empty bags, straw. Slaked lime, i.e. quicklime which has been "slaked" by wetting, is not hazardous.

Magnesium and magnesium alloys. See page 139.

Matches. Lucifer (strike anywhere) matches should be stored in metal-lined cases and safety matches either similarly or in stout wooden cases. In these conditions the risk of a fire originating is small, but fuel would be added to an existing fire.

Metallic powders (often termed "bronze powders") include powdered iron, copper, zinc, magnesium, bronze, and aluminium. Liable to spontaneous combustion, especially if damp, and to be explosive if mixed with air in the form of a dust cloud, or with oxygen carriers. Water must not be used to extinguish a fire involving them.

Methyl acetate, m. alcohol (methanol), m. butyrate, m. cellosolve, etc. Flammable liquids.

Mungo and shoddy are made by tearing up rags and woollen waste, subsequently to be used with new wool in manufacturing woollen cloth. Mungo is made by grinding hard rags such as suitings; shoddy from soft rags such as underclothing or shawls. In each case the rags, before being ground, are dressed with oil, and the material will burn freely. Owing to the cotton fibres present there is a possibility of spontaneous combustion.

Naphtha. A general term for distillates of mineral, rock and tar oils and wood naphtha (methyl alcohol) having flash points up to about 70° F. (21° C.). Flammable liquids. See Chapter VIII.

Naphthalene in the form of crystals is obtained during coal-tar distillation. Used in connection with dye colour making, for manufacturing firelighters in combination with sawdust or shavings, and by furriers as a means of preserving furs against moths. Naphthalene is flammable when heated, especially the crude crystals, the refined product being less dangerous.

Nitrates and nitrites. See oxidizing agents.

Oils may be considered in three classes: Essential oils, fixed oils, and mineral oils.

Essential (or ethereal) oils comprise volatile oils occurring in various parts of plants, chiefly scent-bearing and flavouring products, e.g. lavender, cinnamon, rosemary, peppermint, clove, lemon, juniper, aniseed, camphor, eucalyptus, and turpentine oils. These oils are more dangerous than fixed oils and will burn without a wick. Turpentine is dealt with more fully under that heading.

Fixed oils, i.e. animal and vegetable oils and fats. There is no well-defined difference between fats and oils, the former being rendered liquid by heating. Animal oils include neat's-foot oil, lard, tallow, cod-liver, shark, whale, and porpoise oils; vegetable oils, olive, almond, castor, palm, and coconut, all non-drying oils, and cotton, linseed, poppy, hempseed, tung, rape, or colza, all drying oils.

Apart from the risk of spontaneous combustion, which is vitally affected by the drying properties of the oils (see Chapter VII), there is little difference in the fire hazard. Their flash points are high—well over 300° F. or 150° C.— and they are, therefore, not so easily ignited as the majority of mineral oils. Once alight they burn freely and fiercely, and are difficult to extinguish, as they float on water, the use of which may thus extend the area of the fire.

Mineral and rock oils (hydrocarbons) include petroleum, which is obtained from natural reservoirs beneath the earth's surface, and oils obtained by distillation from bituminous coal or shale. They are not liable to spontaneous combustion; the risks arise from their low flash points. See Chapter VIII.

Oilcakes (cattle cake). Liable to spontaneous combustion.

Oxidizing agents. An oxygen carrier is a chemical compound, including in its composition a large proportion of oxygen, which it will release on the application of a moderate heat. The more important oxidizing agents are—

Chlorate of potash, chlorate of soda, nitrate of potash (nitre or saltpetre), nitrate of soda (cubic nitre or Chili saltpetre), nitrate and perchlorate of ammonia, nitrate of lime; used as artificial manures, and in dye works and explosive factories. Nitrites contain one less oxygen atom than nitrates, and are therefore less active oxidizing agents.

The fire hazards are similar in each case—that, on being heated, oxygen is evolved; that an explosion is probable on coming into contact with burning matter or if water is applied while red hot; that nitric and sulphuric acids in contact cause violent reactions. Mixtures of sulphur and chlorates or nitrates are violently explosive. Chlorates are the more dangerous, and a mixture of chlorate of potash and combustible matter, e.g. if scattered on a wooden floor or mixed with sawdust and straw, etc., can very easily be ignited. A few years ago a serious explosion was caused in such circumstances by a spark from a workman's boot on a stone floor. Empty bags, having contained nitrates, are hazardous, as some nitrate is left between the fibres of the bag and intensifies the likelihood of the fibre spontaneously igniting, especially if damp. Since oxygen carriers do not themselves burn, but are highly dangerous when in contact with any oxidizable matter, and intensify any fire in which they may be heated, the most effective precaution is to store them in a separate building or fire-resisting room reserved for their exclusive storage.

Of other oxidizing agents it may be noted that permanganates are liable to spontaneous combustion if acted on by sulphuric acid; that peroxides will cause spontaneous ignition of organic matter; and that chromates, bichromates, bromates, and perborates possess the general qualities of the class.

Paints. See Varnishes.

Paraffin, Petrol and Petroleum. See Chapter VIII.

Phenol (carbolic acid) gives off flammable vapours when heated.

Phosphorus, white, yellow, or stick, is spontaneously flammable in air at ordinary temperatures, and therefore must be kept under water. When burning gives off dense white poisonous smoke. Easily extinguished with water sprays or wet sand, but will re-ignite on drying. Must be kept wet until removed.

Amorphous, or red, phosphorus is a powder made from white phosphorus, but is much less hazardous; it is not spontaneously flammable in air, but is dangerous in contact with oxygen carriers. Used in the manufacture of matches, etc.

Pitch is the residue from the distillation of tar or petroleum. Used for road-making, caulking boats, and protecting timber against the weather. It does not ignite easily, but will burn freely when warm, giving off dense smoke.

Plastics. This term is applied to organic materials which at some stage of their manufacture are capable of flow, and which by the application of heat and pressure can be caused to take a desired shape and retain it when the applied temperature and pressure are withdrawn. By common consent rubber, glass, pottery and Portland cement are excluded.

There are two main classes: thermoplastics, which can repeatedly be softened by heating and hardened by cooling, e.g. cellulose nitrate, cellulose acetate, and thermosetting plastics, e.g. bakelite which, once set, cannot be again softened by heating. They lend themselves to a wide variety of manufacturing processes, but most plastics are unsuitable for use at high temperatures as they begin to decompose at about 200° C. (392° F.).

It is difficult to grade plastics materials and goods according to their fire hazard because there are differences within each type according to the materials which are mixed with the basic resin. Thus, while there are differences in the burning characteristics, too much emphasis should not be placed on them. All will burn and many give off noxious fumes. Plastics goods are susceptible to damage by heat or smoke.

The dusts of most plastics form explosive mixtures with air.

Celluloid (cellulose nitrate) is in a class by itself. It is hazardous in any form. See Chapter X.

Foamed plastics are made by expanding a plastics material, e.g. polyurethane, polystyrene, to many times its original size by the chemical action of a foaming agent. The products, which are light and provide good sound and heat insulation, are freely used in many industries for insulating, upholstering and packing purposes and as sheets or boards for lining walls and ceilings. They are easily ignited, burn rapidly and fiercely and are extremely difficult to extinguish.

Potassium (metallic) and sodium (metallic) will ignite explosively when heated or when water is applied. Liable to spontaneous ignition in damp air. Can only be stored under mineral oil or in airtight drums. Water, carbon dioxide, carbon tetrachloride, soda acid or foam must not be used for attempts at extinguishment. Dry sand is suitable.

Printers' ink. Cleaning rags contaminated with ordinary printers' ink (which contains lampblack and linseed oil) are liable to spontaneous combustion, and should be kept in metal receptacles pending daily removal.

Photogravure inks, and solutions for cleaning the rollers of machines contain flammable solvents, and such inks should be stored outside the works.

Rags are used in connection with woollen manufacture for making mungo and shoddy. If all were clean the risk would be small, but a few oily cotton rags in a bale or heap may ignite spontaneously and fire the remainder, or a lucifer match mixed with the rags may be ignited by friction. Where rags are ground, precautions against dust explosions should be taken, and against foreign matter, e.g. buttons, likely to cause a frictional spark, being fed into the grinding machines.

Resins and gums. Certain trees exude substances which form hard matter in contact with air. These exudations, particularly those which are soluble in water, are known as gums. Resins are gums which are soluble only in *chemical* solvents, e.g. turpentine, naphtha, methylated spirits. Both are used for making varnishes, electric insulating materials, and have many other uses. When heated they give off flammable vapours, also much smoke, which may damage other goods. The dust of some resins mixed with air is explosive.

Synthetic resins (commonly called plastics) embrace a wide range of products of varied characteristics.

Rubber. Rubber is a gummy substance obtained from certain orders of trees, and is used in the manufacture of waterproof cloth, boots and shoes, motor tyres, electric insulating materials, and many other articles. Burning rubber flows at about 280° C. (536° F.) and while in a molten state gives off volumes of flammable gas and clouds of noxious smoke. Rubber fires are very difficult to extinguish.

Rubber solutions. Rubber may be dissolved in various chemical solvents. The hazards of such solutions depend on the solvent employed: the most hazardous are bisulphide of carbon or ether, but petroleum naphtha is more commonly used, and in all cases flammable vapours are given off. Non-flammable solutions, using carbon tetrachloride as a solvent, are manufactured, but are not so widely used.

Foam rubber may be regarded as similar to foam plastics. It is easily ignited and burns fiercely.

Sawdust is liable to spontaneous combustion if contaminated with vegetable or animal oil, or stored in large high heaps.

Seeds stored in silos swell to such an extent when water is applied that the walls may collapse. Care in extinguishment of fires, even those in adjoining buildings, is therefore necessary. Oily seeds (cotton seed, rape seed, linseed, etc.) are liable to **heat** spontaneously, but whether ignition will occur in the absence of other material is doubtful.

Shoddy. See Mungo and Shoddy.

Sodium. See under Potassium.

Solvents. Many substances used in industry are not soluble in water, and chemical solvents are employed. Most solvents are flammable, including bisulphide of carbon, ether, alcohols, methylated spirits, acetone, amyl acetate, turpentine, petroleum distillates, etc. There are non-flammable solvents, e.g. carbon tetachloride, trichlorethylene, but they are not so widely used on account of their greater cost and toxic properties.

Spirits give off flammable vapours. See under Alcohol and Oils (petroleum).

Sulphur (brimstone) is usually kept in "sticks," or in powder form, known as "flowers of sulphur." It ignites readily and may, in burning, evolve flammable vapours, or, in the form of dust, form an explosive mixture with air. Dangerous when in contact with oxygen carriers, e.g. chlorates and nitrates, friction being sufficient to ignite such mixtures. May ignite spontaneously in contact with lampblack or charcoal. Gives off noxious fumes when burning, and, owing to the low temperature at which it melts, may spread a fire by flowing. Used in making sulphuric acid, fireworks, rubber, and as an insecticide.

Tallow. Melted animal fat, used in soap- and candle-making, and by leather dressers. It is heated before use, and care must be taken that it does not boil over. Makes floors and surroundings greasy, and assists a fire to burn more fiercely. May spread fire by melting and flowing. Floats on water, with which it will not mix. See Oils, fixed.

Tar is distilled from wood, peat, shale, and, most important, coal. It contains flammable products, differing according to the source from which the tar is distilled, and therefore ignites easily and burns fiercely. When coal tar is itself distilled the following products, amongst others, are obtained—

Light spirits or oils: xylol, toluol, benzenes, and naphthas —middle oils: naphthalene, phenol—heavy oils: creosote, anthracene, all of which are hazardous, leaving a residue of pitch.

Thermite is a mixture of iron oxide and powdered aluminium which when burning produces a very high temperature (about 2500° C. or 4532° F.). Used for welding and also as a filling for magnesium incendiary bombs. Cannot be extinguished, either by water or by smothering.

Titanium. The hazards are similar to, but greater than, those of magnesium.

Turpentine. Crude turpentine is an ethereal oil combined with resin obtained from certain trees. When distilled, an oily spirit, oil of turpentine, is produced, leaving a residue of rosin (colophony). Oil of turpentine is used for making or thinning varnish, paints, etc., and is flammable, having a flash point about 90° F. (32° C.).

Turpentine (or turps) substitutes, known as white spirit, are petroleum distillates. Generally they have a slightly lower flash point than turpentine.

Varnishes, lacquers, enamels, and paints are liquids which are used to give to a surface a protective and decorative coating.

Oil varnishes comprise linseed oil, resins, and turpentine. The fire hazard depends largely on the proportion of turpentine. When once alight these varnishes burn freely. Rags soaked in oil varnish may be liable to spontaneous combustion.

Spirit varnishes, which include french polish, consist of resins dissolved in spirit, generally methylated spirit, but some naphtha may be used. Owing to the lower flash point these are more hazardous than oil varnishes.

Enamels are oil varnishes coloured by the addition of pigments.

Paints vary considerably in their composition, but consist mainly of linseed oil, white or red lead, turpentine, and colouring pigments, and will burn freely once ignited.

Synthetic paints or lacquers contain synthetic resins. The solvents are highly flammable and comparable to those used in cellulose paints.

Cellulose paints, lacquers, enamels, and varnishes are hazardous. See Chapter X.

All varnishes, paints, etc., should be stored outside the main buildings, or in a fire-resisting compartment, and sufficient only for one day's use brought into the workshop at a time.

Vegetable fibres and grasses are all hazardous on account of their flammable nature. When loose they ignite easily and burn fiercely and when packed tightly the bales may smoulder for some considerable time before bursting into flames. Some fibres are also liable to spontaneous combustion (see Chapter VII).

Flax (linen, etc., manufacturing), *Hemp* (rope and sailcloth making), and *Jute* (sack and canvas making) are liable to spontaneous combustion if oily. *Hay* is liable to spontaneous combustion if stacked damp.

Cotton. A most important fibre and one of the most hazardous. It will heat if packed damp, but does not ignite spontaneously from this cause. If oily, with vegetable or animal oil, the risk of spontaneous combustion is greater than that of oil in conjunction with any other fibre.

Other important fibres and grasses include—

Alpha, or alfa, esparto (for paper making), *bass or bast, coconut or coir fibre* (for mats), *bamboo fibre* (brush-making), *crin, diss, kapok* (stuffing and upholstering). These are not in themselves liable to spontaneous combustion, but if soaked in vegetable or animal oil may become hazardous in a similar, but lesser, manner to cotton, by reason of sufficient heat being generated by oxidation of the oil to ignite the fibre. Apart from the risk of spontaneous combustion any oily fibre is dangerous because of the ease and fierceness with which it burns.

Fibres should be stored in a separate warehouse, but where this is not practicable care must be taken that oils or fats are not stored near, and that the fibre is not allowed to become wet. Smoking should be prohibited, and all possible sources of ignition eliminated. Water is generally a suitable medium for extinguishing fibre fires, but there is one danger: the fibres swell on becoming wet, and in a warehouse tightly packed the swelling may be sufficient even to cause collapse of the walls.

Man-made fibres vary in their combustibility. Some are regarded as comparable to cotton or natural silk, e.g. Fibro; some as of less hazard, e.g. nylon, Terylene, Ardil, Fibreglass.

Waste. Textile mill waste is oily, easily combustible, and liable to spontaneous combustion. For waste generally see pages 43–5.

Waxes may be the product of the animal, vegetable, or mineral kingdoms, the most important being beeswax and paraffin wax (ozokerite). They are lighter than water, melt on heating to a liquid state, and are combustible. As they are usually too hard to be used as they stand they are mixed with turpentine or other flammable solvent and/or heated prior to use. Many fires have occurred due to the boiling over of waxes being heated over an open fire or gas-ring. Water must not be used in extinguishment, as the burning wax might be spread by floating on the water.

White spirit. See turpentine substitute.

Woodwool. Shredded wood used for packing purposes. Easily ignited and burns fiercely.

Xylol. Flammable liquid, derived from tar and used as a solvent.

APPENDIX

FIRE OFFICES' COMMITTEE STANDARDS OF CONSTRUCTION*

THE Fire Offices' Committee's Standards of Construction are those which have been adopted by the insurance companies, members of the committee, in connection with the classification of buildings for rating purposes. They range from Standard I, which provides very high fire-resistance, to Standard V which is not of a fire-resisting nature. In buildings which conform to Standards I, II or III it is customary to regard each storey as a separate risk for rating purposes.

Standards II and V are reproduced below, Standard II because it is an example of a good class fire resisting building and Standard V because it is on this standard that fire insurance rates are based, discounts off the rates being given for buildings that comply with higher standards.

RULES OF THE FIRE OFFICES' COMMITTEE
FOR
STANDARD II CONSTRUCTION

DEFINITIONS

Brickwork. Solid bricks of burnt clay, concrete (as defined below) or sand lime laid in mortar and/or cement and properly bonded.

Masonry. Stone laid in mortar and/or cement and properly bonded.

Concrete. A mixture composed of Portland or high alumina cement and sand with broken brick, crushed natural stone, blast furnace slag, foamed slag, pumice, well burnt clinker, other similar hard and burnt material or gravel.

Reinforced concrete. The standard of design and construction of reinforced concrete must not be inferior to the recommendations embodied in British Standard Code of Practice CP 114 (1957)—"The structural use of Reinforced Concrete in Buildings."

1. WALLS

(1) External walls to be—

(1) Not less than 9 in. thick, without cavity, of brickwork, masonry and/or concrete.

(2) Cavity walls consisting of two leaves of brickwork each not less than 4½ in. thick with metal ties.

or (3) Not less than 6 in. thick of reinforced concrete.

Non-load bearing panels of brickwork, concrete or reinforced concrete not less than 4 in. thick are allowed.

Glass only, including wired glass and glass bricks, is allowed for window openings.

---

* The standards are revised from time to time and the reader should acquaint himself with any amendments to the rules given in this appendix.

It is recommended that consideration be given to the provision of scuppers in external walls to facilitate the removal of water during fire fighting operations.

(2) Party walls to be not less than 9 in. thick without cavity, going up to or through the roof, and to be of brickwork, masonry, concrete or reinforced concrete.

N.B. Structural metalwork, but not timber, is allowed in external and party walls in conjunction with the foregoing materials provided it is protected in accordance with Rule 5.

2. FLOORS

To be—

(1) Filler joist concrete not less than 5 in. thick. Cover to bottom flanges of joists to be not less than 1 in.

(2) Reinforced concrete not less than 5 in. thick, or

(3) Hollow clay or concrete blocks and concrete, the aggregate thickness of material, i.e. the thickness of solid material in the blocks together with the thickness of concrete, to be not less than $3\frac{1}{2}$ in. The cover to steel reinforcement must be not less than $\frac{3}{4}$ in.

Any supporting walls or piers must be of brickwork, masonry, concrete or reinforced concrete, and any joists, girders, columns or stanchions supporting the floors must be of metal protected in accordance with Rule 5 or of reinforced concrete.

Wood or other material laid on the above described floors allowed provided there is no intervening air space.

It is recommended that floors be made non-porous so that water cannot pass through.

3. FLOOR OPENINGS

Openings in floors for stairs, lifts, or other purposes must be entirely enclosed by walls of—

(i) brickwork not less than $4\frac{1}{2}$ in. thick,

(ii) concrete not less than 4 in. thick,

(iii) reinforced concrete not less than 3 in. thick, or

(iv) hollow clay or concrete blocks not less than 6 in. thick with at least $\frac{1}{2}$ in. of plaster on each side.

every opening from such enclosure to any other part of the building being protected by—

(*a*) a fireproof door conforming to any of the specifications referred to in Sections 1 or 2 of the Committee's Rules for Fireproof Doors, Compartments and Shutters,

(*b*) a door of wrought iron or steel not less than $\frac{1}{8}$ in. thick or a collapsible shutter door of steel not less than $\frac{1}{16}$ in. thick both in wrought iron or steel frames,

(*c*) a door of wood faced on both sides with steel not less than $\frac{1}{16}$ in. thick, or

(*d*) a solid door of wood not less than $1\frac{3}{4}$ in. finished thickness having a wood frame of similar thickness with a rebate of not less than $\frac{1}{2}$ in.

The size of the door opening must not exceed 56 sq. ft. and all doors, other than steel rolling shutters, must be self-closing or be fitted with fastenings engaging into the frame. Panels of wired glass or electro-copper glazing conforming to the Committee's Rules, and not exceeding 4 superficial feet altogether, allowed in each door or leaf in the case of the doors referred to in (a), (b) and (d) above.

Window openings protected by wired glass or electro-copper glazing conforming to the Committee's Rules, or by glass bricks, and not exceeding 16 superficial feet in the aggregate, allowed at each storey in stair enclosures only.

All staircases must have steps and landings wholly of brickwork, masonry, concrete, hollow clay or concrete blocks, and/or metal.

Where the heading of a stair, lift or other enclosure is not formed by part of a roof or floor, it must conform to the requirements for floors.

N.B. The passage through floors of steam, gas or water pipes and of metal or earthenware tubes for electric conductors is allowed provided all pipes and tubes or any enclosing sleeves or collars, which must be incombustible and close fitting, are cemented round the full thickness of the floor.

4. ROOFS

To be—

(1) Filler joist concrete not less than 4 in. thick. Cover to bottom flanges of joists to be not less than $\frac{1}{2}$ in.

(2) Reinforced concrete not less than 4 in. thick, or

(3) Hollow clay or concrete blocks and concrete, the aggregate thickness of material, i.e. the thickness of solid material in the blocks together with the thickness of concrete, to be not less than 3 in. The cover to steel reinforcement must be not less than $\frac{3}{4}$ in.

The following are allowed—

(a) Glass roof lights in incombustible frames.

(b) Open-sided canopies entirely of incombustible construction.

Any supporting walls or piers must be of brickwork, masonry, concrete or reinforced concrete and any joists, girders, trusses, columns and stanchions supporting the roof must be of metal protected in accordance with Rule 5, or of reinforced concrete.

The external surface of the roof, constructed as in (1), (2) or (3) above, may be covered, e.g. for weatherproofing or heat insulating purposes, with

(i) incombustible material,

(ii) asphalt mastic, or

(iii) bituminous roofing laid without intervening air space directly on the structural roof or on incombustible insulating material.

5. PROTECTION OF STRUCTURAL METALWORK

All structural metalwork in or supporting external walls, party walls, floors and roofs, except as otherwise provided for in these Rules, must be completely encased in one of the following forms of protection—

(a) In party walls.

(1) Brickwork, not less than $4\frac{1}{2}$ in. thick with the web hollows filled with concrete and/or brick and mortar.

(2) Concrete not less than $2\frac{1}{2}$ in. thick reinforced centrally with steel mesh or wire.

(3) Foamed slag blocks not less than 4 in. thick and with wire reinforcement in every horizontal joint.

(b) Other than in party walls.

(1) Brickwork not less than 3 in. thick with wire reinforcement in every horizontal joint.

(2) Concrete not less than 2 in. thick reinforced centrally with steel mesh or wire.

(3) Foamed slag blocks not less than 2 in. thick with wire reinforcement in every horizontal joint.

(4) Sprayed asbestos not less than 1 in. thick.

(5) Moulded asbestos not less than $1\frac{1}{2}$ in. thick held in position with nichrome wire.

N.B. Where necessary, protection against mechanical damage is to be provided for columns and stanchions.

NOTE. Building elements of alternative construction may be considered by the Committee for acceptance provided they are constructed of incombustible materials to a design which has been officially tested and accorded a Fire Resistance Grading under British Standard 476 of not less than 2 hours in the case of floors, columns and beams and 1 hour in the case of roofs.

RULES OF THE FIRE OFFICES COMMITTEE
FOR
STANDARD V CONSTRUCTION

BUILDINGS TO BE DEEMED OF STANDARD V CONSTRUCTION MUST CONFORM TO THE FOLLOWING DESCRIPTION

DEFINITIONS

Brickwork. Solid bricks laid in mortar and/or cement.

Masonry. Stone laid in mortar and/or cement.

Hollow blocks ⎫ Hard blocks of well-burned clay or brick-earth, or
Solid blocks ⎬ of cement concrete as defined below.
Slabs ⎭

Concrete. A mixture composed of lime or cement and sand with broken brick, burnt ballast, furnace slag, clinker, other similar hard and burnt material (not including coke breeze), or gravel.

NOTE. "Clinker" must not be used as an aggregate in the composition of concrete that is to be in contact with iron or steel.

Cement concrete. A mixture composed of Portland cement or ciment fondu and sand with broken brick, burnt ballast, furnace slag, clinker, other similar hard and burnt material (not including coke breeze), or gravel.

NOTE. "Clinker" must not be used as an aggregate in the composition of cement concrete that is to be in contact with iron or steel.

WALLS

1. External walls and area walls to be of brickwork, masonry, terra-cotta, cement concrete, hollow blocks, solid blocks and/or slabs.

N.B. Structural iron or steel framework, but not timber framing, is allowed in conjunction with the foregoing materials.

2. Party walls to be of brickwork, masonry, terra-cotta and/or cement concrete and to be not less than 9 in. thick of solid material, devoid of cavity, going up to or through the roof.

N.B. Structural iron or steel framework, but not timber framing, is allowed in conjunction with the foregoing materials provided it be covered with not less than 2 in. of brickwork, masonry, terra-cotta, cement and/or cement concrete.

ROOFS

3. The external covering of the roof to consist of

(1) Concrete. A weatherproofing material on concrete, without intervening air space, is allowed.

(2) Slates (natural or asbestos cement).

(3) Tiles (clay, concrete, asbestos cement, stone or glass).

(4) Wired glass in frames of incombustible material.

(5) Asphalt. The term asphalt includes compounds, of a minimum thickness of $\frac{1}{2}$ in., having a matrix of bitumen or bitumen emulsion with an aggregate or filler of incombustible mineral matter.

(6) Bituminous roofing felt

(a) covered with cement mortar or bitumen macadam not less than $\frac{1}{2}$ in. thick or with sand, ballast, granite or other stone chippings, not less than 2 in. thick, or

(b) on an incombustible deck, with or without a layer of heat-insulating material such as fibre board between the felt and the deck, but without intervening air space. A deck of (i) building slabs consisting of woodwool and an inorganic cementing agent conforming to British Standard 1105: 1961, or (ii) coke breeze concrete, in either case not less than 2 in. in thickness, and surfaced with cement or concrete not less than $\frac{1}{2}$ in. in thickness or with a cement slurry may be considered incombustible for the purpose of this Rule.

NOTE. A deck consisting of metal troughing is allowed provided there is close contact between the deck and the superimposed material for not less than 50 per cent of the roof area and the ends of the cavities are closed with metal.

(7) Asbestos cement sheeting, with or without a metal core.

(8) Metal Sheeting. A coating of bitumen, tar or pitch, or of material impregnated or treated with bitumen, tar or pitch, on the surface which is external to the building is allowed.

N.B. The coating of the underside of a roof with bitumen, tar or pitch, or with material impregnated or treated with bitumen, tar or pitch, is not allowed.

Glass roof lights are allowed.

Roof lights consisting of incombustible rigid plastic or of Fibreglass bonded with a thermosetting resin are allowed provided that

(1) The superficial area of any one light does not exceed 40 sq. ft.

(2) The total superficial area of the lights does not exceed 10 per cent of the superficial area of the roof.

A lantern-attic or lantern light of glass in timber framework raised above the surrounding roof is not allowed.

BIBLIOGRAPHY

The Building Regulations 1965. (Her Majesty's Stationery Office.)
Fire Tests on Building Materials and Structures. (British Standards Institution Specification 476.)
Mitchell's Elementary Building Construction. (B. T. Batsford Ltd.)
Electricity and Fire Risk. E. S. Hodges, F.C.I.I., A.M.I.E.E. (Sir Isaac Pitman & Sons Ltd.)
Chemistry in Relation to Fire Risk. A. M. Cameron, B.Sc., F.I.C. (Sir Isaac Pitman & Sons Ltd.)
Fire Extinguishment and Fire Alarm Systems. J. J. Williamson and P. A. F. Buckle (Sir Isaac Pitman & Sons Ltd.)
Chemical Fires. (Institution of Fire Engineers.)
Regulations for the Electrical Equipment of Buildings. The Institution of Electrical Engineers. (E. & F. N. Spon Ltd.)
Manual of Firemanship. (Her Majesty's Stationery Office.)
The Fire Offices' Committee issue Rules and/or Recommendations in connection with, *inter alia*, the following—

    Automatic fire alarms.
    Automatic sprinklers.
    Computers.
    Drenchers.
    Ethylene gas process of fruit ripening.
    Fireproof doors.
    Fire-resisting construction.
    Grain dryers.
    Grass dryers.
    Liquid fuel for furnaces.
    Magnesium powder and magnesium alloy powder factories.
    Mobile power-driven appliances.
    Nitrate baths used in the heat treatment of aluminium alloys.
    Spraying and other painting processes involving the use of inflammable liquids.

Valuable information may be obtained from the annual reports of the Joint Fire Research Organization, from various memoranda of the Factory Department of the Ministry of Labour published by Her Majesty's Stationery Office and from the quarterly journal and other publications of the Fire Protection Association, Aldermary House, Queen Street, London, E.C.4.

INDEX